CAKES
AND
COWPOKES

CAKES AND COWPOKES

New Desserts from
the Old Southwest

Wayne Harley Brachman

WILLIAM MORROW AND COMPANY, INC.
NEW YORK

Library of Congress Cataloging-in-Publication Data

Brachman, Wayne Harley.
Cakes and cowpokes : new desserts from the Old Southwest / by Wayne
Harley Brachman.
p.   cm.
Includes index.
ISBN 0-688-13091-7
1. Desserts.   2. Cookery, American—Western style.   I. Title.
TX773.B697   1995
641.8´6—dc20   94-38555
CIP

Printed in the United States of America

First Edition

1 2 3 4 5 6 7 8 9 10

ILLUSTRATIONS BY MELANIE PARKS

BOOK DESIGN BY BRIAN MULLIGAN

For Gerald,
who coerced me into the restaurant business.

For Bobby,
who cajoles me to continue in it.

And for Andrea,
who will always be my greatest inspiration.

Acknowledgments

I am not a superstitious type, but there is one mystical embodiment that I do have complete faith in—the fortune cookie. One evening, after a particularly luscious bowl of noodle soup, I had the uncanny good luck to find three of them stuffed into one cookie, in the bottom of the take-out bag. The first said something about my never being sarcastic. After a raucous laugh I caught my breath and opened the second—"You will have grpfgh in your future." This was certainly something to ponder, let alone pronounce. It was the third message that really rang true—"You are blessed with good friends." Everyone involved with this book has been just that, absolutely wonderful friends.

First I would like to thank Harriet Bell, my all-seeing, steadfast, and hilarious editor—boy, did she put up with a lot; my agent, Jane Dystel, who guided, advised, and had faith in me from this book's first inklings; Tom Eckerle, the most brilliant food photographer in the history of the snapshot; and Ceci Gallini who hunted down all those plates and platters.

Thanks to my recipe testers Alix Paley, Bernadette Cura, and Mitch Prensky. Stephanie Leahy and Mario LaVerdiana who helped with the photo shoots. My trusty staff at Mesa Grill and Bolo who donated their ideas, support, and baking efforts: Susan Caprio, Amir Ilan, Kristina Campbel, Lisi Criss, Shuna Leyden, and Miguel Mora. Additional thanks to the many students of the Peter Kump Cooking School who helped to test recipes.

I also want to thank my cooking colleagues: Theresa Scala, Jan Sendel, Katy Sparks, Neil Manacle, Joe Antonishek, and Patrica Yeo; my bosses: Jeff Bliss, Laurence Kretchmer, Jerry Kretchmer, and of course, Dorothy Kretchmer—without their support, none of this would have been possible. Special thanks to Kim Yorio of William Morrow and Kate Krader of *Food & Wine*.

So, who have I left out? Come on, Bobby Flay, I'd have to write a whole chapter to thank you. Yo, you're the best.

Thank you kindly, y'all.

Contents

Introduction

Bake in the Saddle Again

Cowpokes, outlaws, and Apache chiefs, these were the characters who populated the wild frontier of the Southwest. You can still find adventurers out there, but today they are cooks, bakers, and dessert makers and the excitement is being stirred up in their kitchens. Here, in the Southwest, the American food revolution is in high gear. Flavors as bright and bold as the rugged land itself have been harnessed by a new breed of creative chefs, who have reinterpreted them in a sophisticated and colorful cuisine.

The most important kitchen utensil in the Southwest is the melting pot, for it is here that we find the most cross-cultural cooking in the country. Rustic Mexican and classic Spanish meet heartland American and antebellum Southern. Texas alone has an incredible stew pot of cooking cultures, from Cajun, German, Mexican, and Southern to down-home American.

Desserts are a very special part of Southwestern food. After all, they must follow spicy and spectacular main courses—a challenge that no dainty petit four could meet. They must be creative, dramatic, and, above all, irresistibly yummy. Like all contemporary Southwestern foods, desserts are created with an exciting new approach. Time-tested European and American methods are used to refine traditional sweets of the region, while at the same time, classical desserts are re-created with Southwestern ingredients. The result is an explosion of creativity. Traditional Italian biscotti take on a wonderful crunchy texture with the addition of blue cornmeal. Old-fashioned chocolate devil's food cake is reborn, sensuous and mysterious, with a little ancho chile powder. A simple Mexican flan is voluptuous when flavored with luscious chocolate. Experimentation opens up bold, but accessible, new horizons. Southwestern-style chefs soon find that the whole world can be their pantry, as long as the ingredients and the cooking spirit remain bright, light, and bold.

The clear skies, warm weather, and panoramic splendor of the Southwest are reflected in its summery desserts. Whether they are light and fruity ices and salsas or luscious and comforting cakes, they are always straightforward and honest. Flavors combine with an originality that seems to spring up from a mystical source, all-at-once intriguing yet familiar and fun. This cooking may be serious, but it also appeals to the little kid in us.

Over the centuries, different groups have migrated to the Southwest, bringing with them strong new culinary influences. First came nomadic tribes from the north, raiding the pueblos of the Anasazi. Later, the Spanish, Mexicans, "Anglos" arrived, introducing the basic elements that make the area's cooking so unique. To a lesser extent the Cajuns in East Texas, Germans around Austin, Mormons in Utah, and Russian Jews and Italians in Nevada have added their own flavors to the melting pot.

When it comes to dessert, the baking heritage of America shines through. It's here that the great pastries and confections of Europe have been distilled into pure, simple, homey recipes. Pies, cookies, cobblers, puddings, and cakes answer only to one call—that they be delicious. This is what Southwestern desserts are all about: homespun American goodies, with the crunch of cornmeal, an occasional sprinkling of hot chiles and a Spanish and Mexican flair. Like the people of the area, they are straightforward and down to earth, but uniquely individual with a flamboyance all their own.

In the Southwest, flavor comes first. People just don't care about sugar that has been boiled and pulled into silly rock-hard doodads, or chocolate that has been scraped and twisted into fancy-pants frills. Mind you, desserts are brightly hued and spectacular, but theirs is a natural beauty, derived from the resilient colors and textures of fresh fruits, crunchy nuts, and luscious chocolate.

The popularity of the Southwest has spread, and today restaurants specializing in this style of cooking can be found all across the country. It's no surprise that some of the leading chefs on the Southwestern scene are at home cooking on ranges in the concrete canyons of East Coast cities. After all, the most legendary cowgirl of all time, Annie Oakley, never even traveled west of the Mississippi in her entire life.

Southwestern food is no longer relegated to the chili bowl. Today cakes and custards, ice creams, and cobblers can all be made with the area's rustic flavors and imbued with the mystique and allure of this sunny land. They can be a taste adventure as action-packed as any the Wild West has ever known.

Equipment

Aprons, Chaps, Whisks, and Lassos

Besides standard, but high-quality, baking tools, no special equipment is needed for any of the recipes in this book. Here is a checklist of the items that you might need:

Heavy aluminum cookie sheets, preferably with nonstick coating

Rimmed 10- by 15-inch jelly-roll pan

Heavy 8- and 9-inch round cake pans, 9- x 13-inch rectangular pan

9-inch pie pans and $9^{1}/_{2}$-inch tart pans with removable bottoms

Ceramic, glass, or enameled 2-quart baking dish

Ovenproof skillet

Heavy saucepans in a variety of sizes

6-ounce custard cups

Sharp knives

Apple corer

Swivel peeler

Dry and liquid measuring cups

Measuring spoons

Mixing bowls

Rolling pin and a good rolling surface

Wire cooling racks

Rubber and metal spatulas

Slotted steel spoons and wooden spoons

Drum sieve (for sifting flour)

Fine-mesh strainer

Candy thermometer

Ice cream scoops

Pastry brushes

Whisks

Corn bread or madeleine molds

Cookie cutters

In addition, here are a few things that I would be lost without:

It's hard enough to concentrate on one thing at a time, but usually we end up with ten things running at once. An electronic timer will remind you about what's going on in the oven. Some are conveniently made with clips so you can carry them on your apron. Just remember that, of course, the buzzer isn't smart enough to know when the cake is done; it just tells you to take a look and check things out.

Nonstick baker's parchment or Quilon-treated paper pan liners save time in both pan preparation and cleanup. They also help prevent burned bottoms on baked goods of all sorts. Both can be purchased in sheets or rolls and cut to fit the bottoms of cake pans and cookie sheets. Buttered waxed paper can be used as a substitute for lining cake pans but may burn if used on cookie sheets.

When it comes to mixers, nothing beats a powerful stand model with attachments (paddle, whisk, dough hook). It's what I almost always choose because it makes most recipes so much easier. But don't worry, any of the recipes in this book can be made with an electric hand mixer or manual tools.

Ices can be made right in your freezer. For ice cream, however, you have to use a machine specifically designed for the purpose. There are many wonderful types and models on the market. My personal favorite is the old-fashioned barrel and ice churn made by White Mountain of Winchendon, Massachusetts.

Ingredients

Loading the Chuck Wagon

Chiles Fresh chiles with sharp, direct heat are best for dessert: serrano, jalapeño, habanero (Scotch bonnet), or árbol. Always use caution when handling chiles. Wear rubber gloves or coat your hands in oil. Take care to keep your fingers away from your eyes and wash your hands thoroughly. If your fingers still sting, cool them off in a bowl of buttermilk.

Deep, dark ancho chile powder is an essential flavor in Texas chili con carne, but it is also a natural when blended with chocolate. Make sure to buy pure powdered ancho and not a chile blend. And, I've never found two batches with the same heat levels, so taste first and add a pinch of cayenne if you want more heat. Purchase pre-ground ancho chili powder; if you can only find whole dried ancho chiles, cut them into small pieces and grind in an electric coffee grinder.

Chocolate If it's the real thing, it's going to be delicious—but some chocolates are more delicious than others. My personal favorites are Callebaut (Belgium), Valrhona (France), and Van Houten (U.S.).

Always use the type called for in the recipe: unsweetened, bittersweet, semi-sweet, or white. The specific properties (cocoa butter and chocolate liquor content, sweetness) of each have been figured into the recipe.

Mexican chocolate, such as Ibarra, is flavored with cinnamon and almond. It comes in paper-wrapped disks and is available in Spanish markets.

European-style alkalized (Dutch-process) cocoa is a tiny bit sweeter than nonalkalized, but either works equally well.

Citrus Zest When grating citrus zest, make sure to remove only the colored outer layer of skin. Avoid the bitter white pith. Cooking supply stores are full of contraptions for zesting citrus fruits, but I think the best tool is an old-fashioned box grater. Simply scrape the fruit lightly across the fine holes.

Cornmeal Blue cornmeals from New Mexico and smooth-flavored white are almost always ground fine. Yellow cornmeal is available in different grinds. Fine is the most common, but you can also find crunchy coarse grains, often labeled "polenta."

Dried Fruits Often these are interchangeable, so feel free to experiment. Dried sour cherries, blueberries, cranberries, and strawberries are expensive, but they are so intensely flavorful that a little goes a long way. Dried fruits often have to be plumped up in hot liquid and then drained before baking; this process prevents them from scorching in the oven and draining moisture from the dough.

Eggs Use only grade A large eggs for the recipes in this book.

Flour Low-gluten cake flour is the best flour for cakes, but any recipes in this book will work with bleached or unbleached all-purpose flour. Do not, however, under any circumstances, use self-rising flour.

Leaveners   *Baking Powder and Baking Soda* I have never seen single-acting baking powder, but check that yours is double-acting, the type I always use, just in case. It can go stale, so replenish your supply every few months. Baking soda may be lumpy, so always sift it or crumble it up before adding it to other ingredients.

Yeast I prefer fresh (compressed) cake yeast—it's so "alive." It should be proofed in warm (98.6°F) water.

Milk and Cream   Besides good old-fashioned cow juice, I use a lot of buttermilk. Shake well—the thick stuff is on the bottom. I also use goat's milk—it's essential for the Mexican caramel sauce cajeta. It is available at health food and specialty shops.

Look for pasteurized heavy (or whipping) cream. The ultrapasteurized product tastes flat and doesn't combine well in custards.

Any brand of sweetened condensed milk is fine.

Nuts and Seeds   To ensure freshness, buy these in small quantities. Pecans, pine nuts (*piñones*), and shelled unsalted pumpkin seeds (*pepitas*) are the nuts used most frequently in these recipes. Most nuts and seeds are more flavorful if toasted. To do so, spread the nuts or seeds on a cookie sheet and bake for 6 minutes at 350°F, turning the pan once for even toasting. Watch pine nuts particularly carefully, as they can burn and become bitter very easily.

Salt I don't like to use much salt in desserts, but it is necessary in any recipe containing baking powder or whipped egg whites. Always use granulated table salt;

it dissolves quickly and has smaller crystals that will not "cut" strands of egg white protein.

Shortening   Many traditional Southwestern recipes call for lard, but I like to use butter, solid vegetable shortening, or flavorless vegetable oils (corn, soy, or safflower). Unsalted Grade AA butter is the finest and the type you should use.

Spices   Like nuts, spices should be purchased in small quantities to ensure freshness. Anise is a popular flavor, and green anise seeds are called for in Mexican and Southwestern recipes. I prefer the bold flavor of ground Chinese star anise. Try to find canela, also called Mexican cinnamon, to use rather than ordinary supermarket cinnamon. It is slightly milder than regular cinnamon, but it has a lovely, sweet-piquant flavor.

Sweeteners   To measure brown sugar, press it lightly into the measuring cup; it should hold together when turned out.

Piloncillo is a raw Mexican sugar that comes in pylon-shaped chunks. It must be soaked overnight or broken up with a hammer, but the taste is well worth the effort. If you can't find it, substitute dark brown sugar.

Syrups Corn syrup comes in light or dark. Maple comes in grades; I think grade B, which has a deeper flavor, is preferable for baking.

Tequila   Gold, or "reposado," has the richest flavor for desserts.

How to Measure Dry Ingredients

The phone rings, the baby screams . . . it's easy to lose your place in a recipe.

Measure dry ingredients by scooping them up in a metal measuring spoon or cup and then leveling them off with the back of a knife. If the recipe calls for a large amount of a white ingredient (flour, sugar), measure that out first onto a sheet of waxed paper. Measure out colored ingredients (cocoa, cornmeal, cinnamon) in separate spots on top of the white. Finally, measure out any more white ingredients in small quantities (baking powder, salt), partially covering the colored ones. When you return from the telephone, you'll be able to see just what you're up to. Your ingredients will look like the coat of a pinto pony, color-coded right in front of you.

First Things First

Be a smart trail cook. Read recipes through, then assemble all the necessary ingredients and equipment. If you are confronted with a tricky pastry maneuver, you won't get caught in a stampede of flour, butter, and mixing bowls.

Danger

Hot Caramel—Mucho Caliente

Caramel can be dangerous, especially if you are making a sauce with it. Use extreme caution: It is very hot and can stick to your skin. Stand back to avoid splatters, and wear oven mitts to protect your hands. I like to wear painter's gloves when coating molds or cups. In the event that a drop of hot caramel does get on you, quickly dunk the affected part in ice water, then treat as you would any other burn.

CAKES
AND
COWPOKES

CAKES

All-American Butter Cakes,

Or How Chief Sifting Bull Won the West

Versatile and easy, butter cakes are the quintessential American cakes. All sorts of extracts, nuts, and liqueurs can be incorporated into their batters to enhance their rich, buttery flavor.

Making a great cake is all about making great bubbles. Jagged-edged sugar crystals, when beaten into butter at room temperature, cut and form little bubbles. If the butter is too cold, they will be brittle and break. If it's too warm, they will be weak and collapse. Slowly adding eggs creates even more bubbles, building up the volume of the mass. These bubbles are then coated alternately with flour and leavening agents (baking soda and powder) and liquid (buttermilk, coffee, sour cream) to form an adobe-like coating around them. With the introduction of heat comes the release of gases in the leavening agents and expansion of gases trapped in the bubbles. The result is a fluffy, moist cake.

1. For your butter to be "plastic" and capable of forming strong bubbles, it must be at room temperature. Anywhere from 65° to 75°F will do as long as it feels soft and pliable (but not melted). Other ingredients, such as buttermilk and eggs, also work best if they are at close to room temperature.

2. The best flour for cakes is cake flour. It has a low gluten content, so cakes come out fluffier. I have heard of all sorts of tricks for imitating cake flour, but none of them really works. If you can't find it, just substitute all-purpose flour. Even though the package may claim that it is suitable for cakes, never use self-rising flour.

3. It may seem a little tedious, but triple-sifting is worth the effort. Your cakes will be moist and airy with a perfectly crumbly texture. Sifting shuffles the dry ingredients so that they are evenly distributed. It also aerates them so that they fluff up and hold liquids in a coating around the fat bubbles.

4. Add eggs one at a time so they can be smoothly incorporated into the butter and sugar mixture. Beat, beat, beat so your mixture comes up high and light.

5. If necessary, turn your cakes from front to back for even baking, but be extremely careful and don't do it until they are almost done. Cakes are delicate creatures and jostling the pans or banging the oven door may cause them to fall.

6. If the cake starts to pull away from the sides of the pan, remove it from the oven. It has risen to its optimum.

7. Separately baked layers are easier to handle and require much less trimming than baking thicker layers and splitting them. Chill them for easier frosting.

Buttermilk Cake

On its own, Buttermilk Cake is as American as apple pie, but serve it with a fruit salsa (pages 176–185), an ice cream (pages 146–167), or a sauce (pages 186–198), and you've got a Southwestern showstopper. Or just try some Whipped Cream (page 199).

Melted butter or nonstick vegetable spray for greasing the pan

1½ cups cake flour

1 teaspoon baking powder

¼ teaspoon baking soda

½ teaspoon ground cinnamon

¼ teaspoon salt

8 tablespoons (1 stick) unsalted butter, at room temperature

1 cup sugar

2 large eggs, at room temperature

2 tablespoons cream sherry

1 teaspoon vanilla extract

½ cup plus 2 tablespoons buttermilk, at room temperature

1. Set a rack in the middle of the oven and preheat to 375°F. Lightly grease a 9-inch round cake pan. Line it with a disk of parchment paper or buttered waxed paper.

2. Sift the flour, baking powder, baking soda, cinnamon, and salt together onto a sheet of waxed paper. Sift 2 more times to mix and aerate.

continued

3. Put the butter and sugar in the bowl of an electric mixer and beat at high speed for 30 seconds, or until well combined and smooth.

4. Add the eggs one at a time, beating until each is incorporated. Continue beating, scraping down the sides of the bowl if necessary, until light and fluffy, about 5 more minutes.

5. With the mixer on its lowest setting, or using a rubber spatula, beat or fold in one third of the flour mixture. Beat or fold in the sherry, vanilla, and half of the buttermilk, then another one third of the flour mixture. Beat or fold in the remaining buttermilk and then the remaining flour mixture.

6. Spread the batter evenly in the prepared pan. Bake for 30 minutes, or until golden and the center springs back when lightly pressed. Cool the cake in the pan on a wire rack.

Makes one 9-inch cake
Store for up to 3 days, well wrapped, at room temperature.

Papaya Upside-Down Cake

You can bake this in a cake pan but, better yet, bake it right in the skillet you make the topping in. I prefer a stainless steel or aluminum skillet. Cast-iron, although very heat efficient, might be a bit too heavy to flip. Whatever you use, make sure it is completely ovenproof (no plastic or wooden handle or nonstick surface).

6 tablespoons unsalted butter
   plus 8 tablespoons (1 stick),
   at room temperature
1 cup lightly packed dark
   brown sugar
$1/3$ cup (2 ounces) pecan pieces
1 large papaya, peeled,
   halved, seeded, and cut into
   1-inch-thick wedges
$1^1/2$ cups cake flour

1 teaspoon baking powder
$1/4$ teaspoon baking soda
$1/4$ teaspoon salt
$3/4$ cup granulated sugar
2 large eggs, at room
   temperature
2 teaspoons vanilla extract
$1/2$ cup buttermilk, at room
   temperature

1. Set a rack in the middle of the oven and preheat to 375°F.
2. Melt the 6 tablespoons butter in an ovenproof 9-inch skillet over moderate heat. Add the brown sugar and cook, stirring until it is dissolved and bubbling. Remove from the heat. If you are using a 9-inch cake pan, pour the mixture into the pan and swirl it around to coat the bottom evenly; be careful, pardner, this stuff is hot. Sprinkle the pecan pieces over the bottom of the skillet or cake pan.

continued

3. Arrange the papaya wedges in a tight pinwheel around the outside of the pan, and fill in the center with any broken or odd-shaped pieces.

4. Sift the flour, baking powder, baking soda, and salt onto a sheet of waxed paper. Sift 2 more times to mix and aerate.

5. Put the remaining 8 tablespoons butter and the sugar in the bowl of an electric mixer and beat at high speed for 2 minutes, or until well combined and smooth. Add the eggs one at a time, beating until each is incorporated. Continue beating, scraping down the sides of the bowl if necessary, until light and fluffy, about 5 more minutes. With the mixer on its lowest setting, or using a rubber spatula, beat or fold in one third of the flour mixture. Beat or fold in the vanilla and half of the buttermilk, then another one third of the flour mixture. Beat or fold in the remaining buttermilk and then the remaining flour mixture.

6. Spread the batter evenly over the papaya wedges. Bake for 30 minutes, or until golden and the center springs back when lightly pressed. Cool the cake in the pan on a wire rack for 5 minutes.

7. Run a knife around the edge of the pan and place a serving platter on top of the pan. Carefully (no, make that *very carefully*) flip the whole thing over. If any papaya is stuck to the pan, scrape it off with a knife and rearrange on top of the cake. Let cool for 15 minutes before serving.

Makes one 9-inch cake
Store up to 2 days covered in the refrigerator,
but best eaten fresh and warm.

Pecan Cake with Whiskey Praline Frosting

More Cajuns live in Texas than in Louisiana, so pralines, the famous New Orleans candies, are certainly no foreign substance there. Like the candy, this praline frosting sets hard and crumbly, so work quickly. If you have trouble, dip your icing spatula in hot water to warm it.

Melted butter or nonstick
    vegetable spray for greasing
    the pan

Cake

$^1/_2$ cup coarsely chopped
    pecans
$1^1/_4$ cups cake flour
$^3/_4$ teaspoon baking powder
$^1/_4$ teaspoon baking soda
$^1/_4$ teaspoon salt
8 tablespoons (1 stick)
    unsalted butter, at room
    temperature
1 cup sugar

2 large eggs, at room
    temperature
2 teaspoons vanilla extract
$^3/_4$ cup buttermilk

Frosting

$^1/_4$ cup pecan pieces
$^1/_2$ cup heavy cream
8 tablespoons (1 stick)
    unsalted butter
One 16-ounce box ($2^1/_4$ cups
    lightly packed) light brown
    sugar
2 tablespoons bourbon
1 teaspoon vanilla extract

1. Set a rack in the middle of the oven and preheat to 375°F. Lightly grease a 9-inch round cake pan. Line it with a disk of parchment paper or buttered waxed paper.

continued

2. Spread the chopped pecans and the pecan pieces for the frosting on an ungreased cookie sheet, keeping them separate, and toast for 5 minutes, or until golden brown and fragrant.

3. THE CAKE: Sift the flour, baking soda, baking powder, and salt together onto a sheet of waxed paper. Sift 2 more times to mix and aerate.

4. Put the butter and sugar in the bowl of an electric mixer and beat at high speed for 30 seconds, or until well combined and smooth. Add the eggs one at a time, beating until each is incorporated. Continue beating, scraping down the sides of the bowl if necessary, until light and fluffy, about 5 more minutes. With the mixer on its lowest setting, or using a rubber spatula, beat or fold in half of the flour mixture. Beat or fold in the vanilla and half of the buttermilk. Then the remaining flour mixture. Beat or fold in the remaining buttermilk and then the chopped pecans.

5. Spread the batter evenly in the prepared pan. Bake for 30 minutes, or until golden and the center springs back when lightly pressed. Cool the cake in the pan on a wire rack. Turn it out onto a serving platter.

6. THE FROSTING: Combine the cream, butter, and brown sugar in a heavy-bottomed medium saucepan and bring to a boil over high heat, stirring occasionally to help dissolve the sugar. Continue to cook until the syrup reaches 240°F on a candy thermometer. Remove from the heat and carefully (it may splatter) stir in the bourbon, vanilla, and pecans. Let cool for 5 minutes, then beat vigorously with a whisk until light and creamy (about 3 minutes). You may use an electric mixer. Pour the icing over the cake and, using a metal spatula dipped in hot water, spread the icing.

Makes one 9-inch cake that will keep for 3 days, covered.

Blueberry Johnnycakes

Originally called "journey cakes," because of their transportability, these Johnny-cakes should not be confused with the famous Rhode Island pancakes of the same name. Light but rustic, these cornmeal cakes are strictly the kind of dessert that could be turned out of a chuck wagon (provided that it was equipped with an electric mixer and some port wine). They are really a version of the square Utah quick breads that are their other namesakes.

If you have a market that sells different grinds of cornmeal, get some coarse grade for coating the pan. It will add even more crunch. Look for fine yellow cornmeal for the cake batter.

Melted butter for greasing the pan
$1/4$ cup yellow cornmeal, preferably coarse, for coating the pan
2 cups cake flour
$1^1/2$ teaspoons baking powder
$1/2$ teaspoon baking soda
$1/4$ teaspoon salt
12 tablespoons ($1^1/2$ sticks) unsalted butter, at room temperature

$1^1/2$ cups sugar
3 large eggs, at room temperature
$3/4$ cup buttermilk
1 tablespoon vanilla extract
$3/4$ cup fine yellow cornmeal
$1/4$ cup port
1 pint blueberries

continued

1. Set a rack in the center of the oven and preheat to 375°F. Liberally butter a 9- by 13-inch cake pan, and coat with the ¼ cup cornmeal, shaking out the excess.

2. Sift the flour, baking powder, baking soda, and salt together onto a sheet of waxed paper. Sift 2 more times to mix and aerate.

3. Put the butter and sugar in the bowl of an electric mixer and beat at high speed for 30 seconds, or until smooth and well combined. Add the eggs one at a time, beating until each is incorporated. Continue beating, scraping down the sides of the bowl if necessary, until light and fluffy, about 5 more minutes. With the mixer on its lowest setting, or using a rubber spatula, beat or fold in half of the flour mixture. Beat or fold in the buttermilk and vanilla and then the fine cornmeal. Beat or fold in the port, then the remaining flour mixture, and, finally, the blueberries.

4. Carefully spread the batter in the pan, taking care not to disturb the cornmeal. Bake for 35 minutes, or until golden and the center springs back when lightly pressed. Cool the cake in the pan on a wire rack.

5. To serve, cut into 3-inch squares. Invert the pieces onto serving plates, so the berry-studded crunchy bottom crust becomes the top.

Makes twelve 3-inch squares
Store for up to 3 days, well wrapped, at room temperature.

Banana Layer Cake with Peanut Butter Buttercream

None of the beautiful geological formations in the Southwest would exist if it weren't for sedimentation, or, more specifically, the erratic erosion of the varied strata of sedimentary rock. The results of this process are breathtaking canyons, buttes, and mesas.

Not to be outdone by Mother Nature, this layer cake is spectacular in its own right, with strata of banana cake and peanut butter frosting that run vertically instead of horizontally.

Banana Cake

2^1/2 cups cake flour

1 teaspoon baking soda

^{1}/4 teaspoon baking powder

^{1}/4 teaspoon salt

12 tablespoons (1^1/2 sticks) unsalted butter, at room temperature

1^1/4 cups sugar

3 large eggs, at room temperature

3 large very ripe bananas

^{1}/2 cup sour cream

1 tablespoon vanilla extract

Peanut Butter Buttercream

8 ounces (2 sticks) unsalted butter, at room temperature

One 18-ounce jar creamy peanut butter

2^1/2 cups confectioners' sugar

Decorations

^{1}/2 cup unsalted peanuts plus ^{1}/2 cup chopped unsalted peanuts

1 ounce semisweet chocolate, melted

continued

13

1. THE CAKE: Set a rack in the middle of the oven and preheat to 375°F. Lightly grease the sides of two 15^1/$_2$- by 10^1/$_2$-inch jelly-roll pans. Line them with parchment or buttered waxed paper.

2. Sift the flour, baking soda, baking powder, and salt together onto a sheet of waxed paper. Sift 2 more times to mix and aerate.

3. Put the butter and sugar in the bowl of an electric mixer and beat at high speed for 30 seconds, or until well combined and smooth. Add the eggs one at a time, beating until each is incorporated. Continue beating, scraping down the sides of the bowl if necessary, until light and fluffy and doubled in volume, about 5 more minutes.

4. In a small bowl, using the mixer or a fork, mash the bananas until soupy. Stir in the sour cream and vanilla.

5. With the mixer on its lowest setting, or using a rubber spatula, beat or fold one third of the flour mixture into the butter mixture. Beat or fold in half of the banana mixture, then another one third of the flour mixture. Beat or fold in the remaining banana mixture and then the remaining flour mixture.

6. Divide the batter between the prepared pans, spreading it evenly with an offset metal spatula. Bake for 15 minutes; or until just golden and the centers spring back when lightly pressed. Cool the cakes in the pans on wire racks.

7. THE BUTTERCREAM: Put the butter and peanut butter in the bowl of an electric mixer, and beat at medium speed until blended. Reduce the speed to low and gradually beat in the sugar. Increase the speed to medium and beat for 3 minutes, or until smooth and fluffy.

8. Cover each cake with a sheet of waxed paper or parchment paper. Place a large baking sheet over one cake, and carefully flip the cake over. Peel off the parchment. With a serrated knife or a pizza wheel, trim the edges of the cake. Using

a ruler as a guide, cut ten 2-inch by 15-inch strips from the cake. Repeat with the second cake. Reserve one third of the buttercream, and spread the remaining buttercream evenly over the cake strips.

9. Disassemble a 9-inch springform pan, and wrap the bottom in plastic wrap. Tightly roll one cake strip up like a jelly roll, and stand it on end in the center of the pan bottom. Coil the remaining strips around the first, butting the ends together to form one large spiral. Fit the sidepieces of the springform on and snap it closed. Freeze for at least 4 hours, or overnight.

10. THE DECORATIONS: Arrange the whole peanuts in little clusters on a plate covered with waxed paper. Melt the chocolate in a small bowl set over a saucepan of barely simmering water, and using a fork, drizzle the chocolate over the peanuts. Refrigerate for 15 minutes to set.

11. Soak a towel in hot water and squeeze dry. Wrap it around the springform to loosen the sides. Remove the sides of the pan and invert the cake onto a serving platter or cardboard cake round. Using a metal spatula, frost the top and sides of the cake with the reserved buttercream. Press the chopped peanuts into the sides of the cake, and decorate the top with peanut clusters. Serve at room temperature.

Makes one 9-inch cake
Store for up to 3 days, covered, in the refrigerator.

15

Ancho Chile Devil's Food Cake

Angel food cake is light and angelic, but regular devil's food cake, although quite delicious, doesn't have the fire to justify its name. You can devilishly change that, however, by adding a little powdered ancho, mildest of the dried chiles, and a pinch of cayenne to give it just enough of a spicy edge.

Hot spices and chocolate are not newfangled concepts. Back in the early 1600s, it was quite the rage to guzzle chocolate beverages thickly laced with black and/or "Mexican" pepper.

Melted butter or nonstick
   vegetable spray for greasing
   the pan
$1^1/_4$ cups cake flour
$^1/_2$ cup unsweetened cocoa
   powder
3 tablespoons pure ancho chile
   powder (see Note)
$^1/_8$ teaspoon cayenne
1 teaspoon baking soda
$^1/_4$ teaspoon baking powder

$^1/_2$ teaspoon salt
10 tablespoons unsalted butter,
   at room temperature
$1^1/_2$ cups sugar
3 large eggs, at room
   temperature
1 teaspoon vanilla extract
$^1/_2$ cup buttermilk, at room
   temperature
$^1/_2$ cup hot coffee
1 recipe Ganache (page 18)

1. Set a rack in the middle of the oven and preheat to 350°F. Lightly grease two 9-inch cake pans and line them with disks of parchment paper or greased waxed paper.

2. Sift the flour, cocoa, ancho chile powder, cayenne, baking soda, baking powder, and salt onto a sheet of waxed paper. Sift 2 more times to mix and aerate.

3. Put the butter and sugar in the bowl of an electric mixer and beat at high speed for 30 seconds, or until well combined and smooth. Add the eggs one at a time, beating until each is incorporated. Continue beating, scraping down the sides of the bowl if necessary, until light and very fluffy, about 5 more minutes. With the mixer on its lowest setting, or using a rubber spatula, beat or fold in one third of the flour mixture. Beat or fold in the vanilla, half of the buttermilk, and half of the coffee, then another one third of the flour mixture. Beat or fold in the remaining buttermilk and coffee, then the remaining flour mixture.

4. Spread the batter evenly in the prepared pans. Bake for 30 minutes, or until the centers spring back when lightly pressed. Cool the cake layers in the pans on a wire rack.

5. Invert each cake onto a plate. Trim the tops flat with a serrated knife. Spread one third of the ganache over one layer. Flip the other layer on top, and frost the top and sides of the cake with the remaining ganache.

**Makes one 9-inch cake
Store for up to 3 days in the refrigerator.**

Note: Ancho chile powder is available in Mexican groceries. See Mail Order Sources, page 209. Don't even try to use the mixed chile powder found in supermarkets or you will end up with a cake that tastes like dirt.

Ganache

6 ounces semisweet chocolate,
coarsely chopped

³/₄ cup heavy cream

1. Put the chocolate in a small bowl. In a small saucepan, bring the cream to a scald over medium heat. Pour the hot cream over the chocolate. Working from the center out, gently stir to melt and blend until smooth. Let the ganache sit until slightly thickened, about 10 minutes; it should be spreadable but still pourable.

Makes enough to frost one 9-inch cake

Note: If your ganache doesn't have a smooth patina, blend in a few drops of cold heavy cream. A matte finish will dry to a mirror shine.

Petrified Forest Chocolate Cake

In 1852, Samuel German, an employee of Walter Baker & Company, invented the chocolate blend that now bears his name. (So it was just coincidence that Walt's last name was Baker, and German sweet chocolate has nothing to do with the country.) They promoted their product with a German's Chocolate Cake with a coconut and brown sugar frosting. Our Petrified Forest Chocolate Cake uses a similar frosting and some ancho chile, but dried cherries make it a play on the classic German Black Forest cake as well.

2 cups (scant 6 ounces) dried shredded coconut

2 Ancho Chile Devil's Food Cake layers (page 16)

One 16-ounce box (2^1/4 cups lightly packed) light brown sugar

^{1}/4 cup dark corn syrup

^{1}/2 cup water

6 large egg whites

Pinch of salt

1 teaspoon granulated sugar

2 teaspoons vanilla extract

^{1}/2 cup (2^1/2 ounces) dried cherries, soaked in ^{1}/2 cup hot water for 20 minutes and well drained

1. Preheat the oven to 350°F.
2. Spread the coconut on a baking sheet and toast in the oven for 7 minutes: Turn the pan for even browning, but aim for some variation in color, from white to tan to brown. Let cool.

continued

3. Turn each cake layer upside down onto a plate. Trim the tops flat with a serrated knife.

4. Combine the brown sugar, corn syrup, and water in a medium heavy-bottomed saucepan. Bring to a boil over high heat, stirring a few times to help dissolve the sugar crystals, and boil until the syrup registers 240°F on a candy thermometer.

5. Meanwhile, in an immaculately clean, dry mixing bowl of an electric mixer, combine the egg whites and salt, and whisk until soft peaks form. Sprinkle on the granulated sugar and whisk until the peaks stiffen to the consistency of shaving cream.

6. Whisking constantly, carefully drizzle the hot syrup into the egg whites. Add the vanilla, and whisk until thickened and spreadable.

7. With a rubber spatula, fold 1½ cups of the coconut into the frosting. Transfer one quarter of the frosting to a small bowl, and stir in the drained cherries. Spread this over one cake layer. Flip the other layer on top, and frost the top and sides of the cake with the remaining frosting. Gently press the remaining ½ cup coconut into the sides of the cake.

Makes one 9-inch cake
Store for up to 2 days refrigerated.

Rio Grande Mud Pie

This flourless "mud pie" is denser, richer, and more chocolaty than most chocolate cakes three times its size, so cut small slices. Fruits from north and south of the border turn it into a bright, summery dessert.

Melted butter or nonstick
vegetable spray for greasing
the pan

Cake

8 ounces bittersweet chocolate,
coarsely chopped
8 tablespoons (1 stick)
unsalted butter, cut into
pieces
3 large eggs, at room
temperature
2 tablespoons sugar

1 quart ice cream (Mango,
page 163; Canela, page
162; Serrano, page 158;
Piloncillo, page 152; or
Banana Chocolate Crackle,
page 154)
1 recipe Tia Maria Chocolate
Sauce (page 188)
1 mango, peeled and cut into
$1/2$-inch chunks (see
page 164)
1 papaya, peeled, seeded, and
cut into $1/2$-inch chunks
$1/2$ pint raspberries,
blackberries, or strawberries
2 cactus pears, peeled and cut into
bite-sized chunks (see Note), or
any combination of fruit

1. Set a rack in the middle of the oven and preheat to 350°F. Lightly grease a 9-inch round cake pan. Line it with a disk of parchment paper or buttered waxed paper.

continued

2. Melt the chocolate and butter in a small bowl set over a saucepan of barely simmering water, stirring until smooth. Remove from the heat and set aside in a warm place.

3. Put the eggs and sugar in a large bowl and set it over the simmering water. Increase the heat slightly, and whisk until the eggs are as warm as bathwater; don't let them scramble.

4. Remove the eggs from the heat and continue whisking (you can switch to an electric mixer) until they are fluffy and form soft peaks. Fold in the melted chocolate mixture in 3 additions. Spread the batter evenly in the prepared pan.

5. Set the cake pan in a roasting pan and add hot water to come halfway up the sides of the cake pan. Bake for 10 minutes, then cover both pans with foil and bake for 25 minutes longer. Remove from the water bath and let cool on a rack until firm, about 3 to 4 hours.

6. Invert the cake onto a serving platter. Having trouble? Pop it back in the oven for 2 minutes.

7 . To serve, mound the ice cream on top of the cake. Drench with Tia Maria Chocolate Sauce and garnish with the fruit.

Makes one 9-inch cake
Store for up to 3 days refrigerated, well wrapped.

Note: Look for dark red prickly pears (sometimes called tuna). With a small knife, slice off the ends. Slit the skin from end to end and stab the fruit with a fork. While rolling the fruit toward you with the fork, slice and pull the skin away with the knife.

Mexican Gold Nugget Brownie Torte

Gold is actually edible. I am not advocating that you make soup out of your grand-father's pocket watch, but a tiny sprinkling of twenty-two-karat gold dust, although flavorless, can be quite dramatic looking. This brownie, leavened with egg white, is, in reality, a very elegant chocolate walnut torte.

Melted butter or nonstick
   vegetable spray for greasing
   the pan
4 ounces bittersweet chocolate,
   coarsely chopped
1/2 cup strong coffee
3/4 cup plus 1 teaspoon sugar
6 tablespoons unsalted butter,
   at room temperature
6 large eggs, separated

1 1/2 cups coarsely chopped
   walnuts
2 tablespoons dried bread
   crumbs
Pinch of salt
1 recipe Ganache (page 18)
1 disk Ibarra chocolate,
   coarsely chopped (see Notes)
1/2 gram 22-karat gold dust
   (see Notes)

1. Set a rack in the middle of the oven and preheat to 350°F. Lightly grease a 9-inch round cake pan. Line it with a disk of parchment paper or buttered waxed paper.

2. Place the bittersweet chocolate in a medium bowl. Combine the coffee and 1/2 cup of the sugar in a small saucepan. Heat over medium heat, stirring, until the

sugar is completely dissolved. Pour the hot sugar syrup over the chocolate, and stir until melted and smooth.

3. Put the butter and $^1/_4$ cup of the sugar in the bowl of an electric mixer and beat at high speed for 2 minutes, or until well combined and smooth. Add the eggs one at a time, beating until each is incorporated. Continue beating, scraping down the sides of the bowl if necessary, until light and fluffy, about 5 more minutes. With the mixer on its lowest setting, or using a rubber spatula, gradually beat or fold in the chocolate syrup. Beat or fold in the nuts and bread crumbs.

4. In an immaculately clean, dry bowl, combine the egg whites and salt and whisk until soft peaks form. Sprinkle on the remaining teaspoon sugar and whisk until the peaks stiffen to the consistency of shaving cream. Fold one third of the egg whites into the chocolate mixture, and then gently but thoroughly fold in the rest of the whites.

5. Spread the batter in the prepared pan. Bake for 50 minutes, or until springy to the touch and a cake tester comes out clean. Cool in the pan on a wire rack.

6. Turn the cake out onto a wire rack. Pour the ganache over it and, using as few strokes as possible, frost the cake.

7. Scatter the Ibarra chocolate over the top of the cake, then use a fine strainer to sprinkle the gold dust over it.

Makes one 9-inch cake
Store for up to 3 days, at room temperature.

Notes: Used primarily to make hot chocolate, Ibarra, a blend of cocoa, almonds, and cinnamon, is sold in Latin American groceries.

Gold dust is available at cake decorating shops. (For further information, see Mail Order Sources, page 209.)

Colorado Carrot Cake

The Old Southwest was a land of nomads: Navajos, cowboys, and, in the mountains of Colorado, trappers. Foraging in the Rockies was sometimes tricky and they couldn't carry very much with them, so dried fruits became a staple of the mountain men. "Grizzly Wayne's" Colorado Carrot Cake is chock-full of a variety of dried fruits.

Melted butter or nonstick vegetable spray for greasing the pan

Cake
3/4 cup dried fruit (pineapple, apricots, cherries, and/or peaches in any combination), chopped into 1/4-inch pieces
3/4 pound carrots, peeled
1 cup cake flour
1 teaspoon baking soda
1 teaspoon baking powder
1/2 teaspoon cinnamon
1/2 teaspoon salt
3/4 cup sugar
2 large eggs, at room temperature
3/4 cup vegetable oil
2 teaspoons vanilla extract
1/2 cup chopped pecans

Frosting
12 ounces cream cheese, at room temperature
3/4 cup confectioners' sugar
1 tablespoon vanilla extract
1 tablespoon bourbon

1. THE CAKE: Set a rack in the middle of the oven and preheat to 350°F. Lightly grease a 9-inch round cake pan. Line it with a disk of parchment paper or buttered waxed paper.

continued

2. Put the dried fruit in a small saucepan with enough water to cover, and bring to a boil. Remove from the heat and let stand for 3 minutes; drain.

3. Chop the carrots in a food processor fitted with the metal blade or grate on a hand grater.

4. Sift the flour, baking soda, baking powder, cinnamon, and salt together onto a sheet of waxed paper. Sift 2 more times to mix and aerate.

5. Put the sugar and eggs in the bowl of an electric mixer and beat at high speed for 2 minutes, or until creamy. While beating, slowly drizzle in the oil until well blended and emulsified. With the mixer on its lowest setting, or using a rubber spatula, fold in one third of the flour mixture. Beat or fold in the carrots and vanilla, then another one third of the flour mixture. Beat or fold in the dried fruit, then the remaining flour mixture and the pecans.

6. Spread the batter evenly in the prepared pan. Bake for 45 minutes, or until the center springs back when lightly pressed and a cake tester comes out clean. Cool the cake in the pan on a wire rack, then turn it out onto a serving platter.

7. THE FROSTING: Put the cream cheese, confectioners' sugar, vanilla, and bourbon in the bowl of an electric mixer. Beat at low speed until blended, then increase the speed and beat until fluffy. Using a metal spatula, frost the cake.

Makes one 9-inch cake
Store for up to 3 days in the refrigerator.

Gingerbread

This is the thick, gooey, tasty kind of gingerbread, not that pastry Sheetrock that is used to construct those adorable but, let's face it, inedible chalets and figures.

Blackstrap molasses is available at health food stores. It's the stuff that has spawned phrases like "thick as . . ." and "slow as . . . ." You can end up spending a good part of an afternoon trying to pour it out, so to speed things along, set the bottle in hot water for about twenty minutes to loosen it up. Don't even try to use the thin supermarket-type molasses in this recipe—it just won't work.

Serve Gingerbread with Apple-Walnut Salsa (page 183), Canela Ice Cream (page 162), and/or Whiskey Butterscotch Sauce (page 193).

*Melted butter or nonstick
    vegetable spray for greasing
    the pan
One 3-inch piece fresh ginger,
    peeled
1 teaspoon ground ginger
2^1/$_2$ cups cake flour
1^1/$_2$ teaspoons baking soda
1 teaspoon cinnamon
1 teaspoon ground cloves
^{1}/$_2$ teaspoon salt*

*8 ounces (2 sticks) unsalted
    butter, at room temperature
^{3}/$_4$ cup sugar
1 large egg, at room
    temperature
^{1}/$_2$ cup blackstrap molasses
    (see above)
^{1}/$_2$ cup plus 2 tablespoons hot
    water
^{1}/$_2$ teaspoon vanilla extract*

continued

1. Set a rack in the middle of the oven and preheat to 350°F. Lightly grease a 9-inch round cake pan. Line it with a disk of parchment paper or buttered waxed paper.

2. Grate the ginger (with a box or hand grater) to produce about 1 tablespoon of paste. Use the ground ginger to "mop up" any juice that has splattered around.

3. Sift the flour, baking soda, cinnamon, cloves, and salt onto a sheet of waxed paper. Sift 2 more times to mix and aerate.

4. Put the butter and sugar in the bowl of an electric mixer and beat at high speed for 2 minutes, or until well combined and smooth. Beat in the egg. Continue beating, scraping down the sides of the bowl if necessary, until light and fluffy, about 5 more minutes. Beat in the grated and ground ginger.

5. In a small bowl, mix together the molasses, hot water, and vanilla. With the mixer on its lowest setting, or using a rubber spatula, beat or fold one third of the flour mixture into the butter mixture. Beat or fold in half of the liquid ingredients, then another one third of the flour mixture, and then the remaining liquid. Beat or fold in the remaining flour mixture.

6. Spread the batter evenly in the prepared pan. Bake for 35 minutes, or until the center springs back when lightly pressed. Cool the cake in the pan on a wire rack.

Makes one 9-inch cake
Store for up to 3 days, well wrapped, at room temperature.

Note: Don't throw the ginger into a food processor and think that everything will be just fine. Hand grating is a little more tiresome, but the processor will leave you with a stringy mess.

Sticky Buns and Ice Cream

Is there anyone out there who can't confess to having ice cream first thing in the morning, at least once? Although we would never admit it, along with cold pizza and leftover Chinese takeout, ice cream is probably one of the most popular breakfasts in America. So, pick your flavor, because a scoop of any ice cream can turn one of these pecan- and caramel-coated sticky buns into a gooey dessert or a sensational main course at brunch time.

Present these sticky buns as a whole cake, breaking off individual pieces for each serving.

Dough

$1/2$ cup lukewarm milk

$1/2$ ounce fresh (compressed) yeast or one $1/4$-ounce package active dry yeast

$1/4$ cup sugar

2 large eggs, at room temperature

$1/2$ teaspoon salt

3 cups all-purpose flour

4 tablespoons unsalted butter

Sticky Topping

4 tablespoons unsalted butter

$3/4$ cup packed dark brown sugar

$3/4$ cup (4 ounces) pecan pieces

Cinnamon Filling

2 tablespoons unsalted butter, melted

$1/4$ cup sugar

1 tablespoon cinnamon

Ice cream (any flavor) for serving

continued

1. THE DOUGH: Combine the milk, yeast, and sugar in the bowl of an electric mixer and let rest for a few minutes to proof.

2. Mix the eggs and salt into the yeast mixture. With a dough hook, blend in the flour. Then blend in the butter by the tablespoonful. With the dough hook, beater, knead the dough for 7 minutes, or until springy and elastic. Transfer the dough to a lightly oiled bowl, cover with plastic wrap, and set aside in a warm place until doubled in volume, about 50 minutes.

3. THE TOPPING: Lightly butter the bottom of a 9- x 13-inch baking pan. In a small saucepan, combine the butter and brown sugar and cook, stirring until the sugar has dissolved. Pour the mixture into the pan and sprinkle the pecan pieces over it.

4. Punch down the dough. On a lightly floured surface, roll it out into an 8- by 18-inch rectangle. Brush with the melted butter and sprinkle on the cinnamon and sugar. Starting at a long side, roll the dough up into a log. Slice into twelve 1$^1/_2$-inch-wide rolls. Lay them, cut side down, in the cake pan, squeezing them in if necessary. Let rise in a warm place until doubled in volume, about 50 minutes.

5. Set a rack in the middle of the oven and preheat to 350°F.

6. Bake the rolls for 30 to 35 minutes, or until golden brown. Carefully invert onto a serving platter and let cool for just a few minutes. Break into individual buns and serve warm, with ice cream.

Makes 12 buns
Store for up to 1 day, well wrapped, at room temperature
or freeze for up to 2 months.

Three Cheesecakes

In the late 1940s, a glamorous gangster named Bugsy Siegel dreamed up what was to become the gambling capital of America: Las Vegas, Nevada. Like their predecessors, Apache raiders, Spanish conquistadors, Mexican fortune hunters, and "Anglo" desperadoes, Bugsy and his cohorts invaded with fast guns, dreams of quick bucks, and their own favorite ethnic foods—making cheesecake as integral to Nevada cuisine as tacos are to Texas.

Southwestern cheesecake is like New York cheesecake and should be dense and luscious with a real knockout punch of flavor. Don't settle for anything more subtle than a bulldozer.

1. Good cheesecake takes time, so plan ahead. Take your cream cheese and butter out well in advance (early in the morning or even the night before) so they can warm up to room temperature. Cold cream cheese makes lumpy cheesecake.

2. Mix the batter slowly to avoid air bubbles.

3. Bake slowly and cool slowly. Keep an eye on the cake to make sure it doesn't puff up too fast: If necessary, turn the oven down to 275°F or even 250°F and bake longer than the recipe specifies.

4. It's trickier to release a cheesecake from a one-piece pan, but springforms, even if completely sealed in foil, can still spring leaks. To release a cheesecake from a one-piece pan, pop the cake into a hot (300° to 375°F) oven for two minutes. Invert the cake onto a plate covered with plastic wrap or foil. Shake the pan: Aha, it releases! Now, flip the cheesecake over onto a serving plate so it is right side up again. For the springform, simply pop it in the oven for two minutes, unspring . . . voilà, uh, I mean, caramba!

Whiskey Cheesecake with Pumpkin Seed Crust

Whiskey is a truly wonderful flavor for desserts, and the baking process cooks out most of the alcohol. In Mexico, pumpkin seeds, or *pepitas*, are used in a variety of dishes from sauces to cookies. You can use either an 8- by 3-inch one-piece cake pan or an 8- by 2½-inch springform pan wrapped watertight in two layers of foil.

1 tablespoon unsalted butter, melted, for greasing the pan

Crust
½ cup shelled pumpkin seeds
1 cup graham cracker crumbs
2 tablespoons sugar
6 tablespoons unsalted butter, melted

Cake Batter
1½ pounds cream cheese, at room temperature
6 tablespoons unsalted butter, at room temperature
1 cup sugar
2 tablespoons cornstarch
4 large eggs, at room temperature
1 cup sour cream
¼ cup bourbon
2 teaspoons vanilla extract

1. Set a rack in the middle of the oven and preheat to 300°F. Grease the cake pan or springform with the melted butter.

2. THE CRUST: Spread the pumpkin seeds on a cookie sheet and toast in the oven for 6 minutes, or until you hear them pop for 2 minutes. Turn the pan once for even toasting.

3. Combine the graham cracker crumbs, sugar, and toasted pumpkin seeds in a medium bowl. Add the melted butter and blend well. Pat the mixture gently and evenly over the bottom of the prepared pan.

4. THE BATTER: Put the cream cheese, butter, sugar, and cornstarch in a mixing bowl and beat at medium speed just to blend; take care not to beat too much air into the batter. Add the eggs one at a time, beating until each is incorporated. Reduce the speed and beat in the sour cream, bourbon, and vanilla.

5. Pour the batter into the prepared pan. Set the pan in a larger pan, such as a roasting pan, and pour about an inch of hot water into the larger pan. Bake for 1 hour and 15 minutes to $1^1/_2$ hours, or until lightly tanned, slightly puffed, and barely firm. Cool to room temperature in the water bath. Then remove from the water bath and refrigerate overnight.

6. Remove the cake from the pan, following the instructions on page 31.

Makes one 8-inch cake
Store for up to 4 days, wrapped, in the refrigerator.

Dried Blueberry Cheesecake with Pecan Crust

Dried blueberries are intensely flavorful and worth hunting for. Inexpensive port works fine here, so don't bother with the good stuff. You can use either an 8- by 3-inch one-piece cake pan or an 8- by 2$^{1}/_{2}$-inch springform pan wrapped watertight in two layers of foil.

1 tablespoon unsalted butter, melted, for greasing the pan

Crust

$^{1}/_{2}$ cup pecan pieces
1 cup graham cracker crumbs
2 tablespoons sugar
6 tablespoons unsalted butter, melted

Cake Batter

$^{1}/_{2}$ cup port
$^{3}/_{4}$ cup (4 ounces) dried blueberries

1$^{1}/_{2}$ pounds cream cheese, at room temperature
6 tablespoons unsalted butter, at room temperature
1 cup sugar
2 tablespoons cornstarch
4 large eggs, at room temperature
1 cup sour cream
2 teaspoons vanilla extract

Glaze

$^{1}/_{4}$ cup port
$^{1}/_{4}$ cup blueberry preserves

1. Set a rack in the middle of the oven and preheat to 300°F. Grease the cake pan or springform with the melted butter.

2. THE CRUST: Spread the pecans on a cookie sheet and toast in the oven 8 minutes or until fragrant, turning once for even toasting.

3. Combine the graham cracker crumbs, sugar, and toasted pecans in a medium bowl. Add the melted butter and mix well. Pat the mixture gently and evenly over the bottom of the prepared pan.

4. THE BATTER: In a small saucepan, combine the port and blueberries and bring to a boil. Reduce the heat and simmer for 3 minutes. Remove from the heat and set aside.

5. Put the cream cheese, butter, sugar, and cornstarch in a mixing bowl and beat at medium speed just to blend; take care not to beat too much air into the batter. Add the eggs one at a time, beating until each is incorporated. Reduce the speed and beat in the sour cream and vanilla. Beat in the blueberries, with their liquid.

6. Pour the batter into the prepared pan. Set the pan in a larger pan, such as a roasting pan, and pour about an inch of hot water in the larger pan. Bake for 1 hour and 15 minutes to 1½ hours, or until lightly tanned, slightly puffed, and firm. Cool to room temperature in the water bath. Then remove from the water bath and refrigerate.

7. Remove the cake from the pan, following the instructions on page 31.

8. THE GLAZE: Combine the port and preserves in a small saucepan and bring to a boil. Boil, stirring, until the preserves are melted, 3 to 4 minutes. Strain through a fine sieve, then drizzle over the top of the cake. Refrigerate for 10 minutes to set before serving.

Makes one 8-inch cake
Store for up to 3 days, loosely wrapped, in the refrigerator.

Dried Cherry-Vanilla Cheesecake with Sesame Seed Crust

The cherries show through the top of this cake so that it looks pretty even without a glaze. You can use an 8- by 3-inch one-piece cake pan or an 8- by 2¹/₂-inch spring-form wrapped watertight in two layers of foil.

1 tablespoon unsalted butter, melted, for greasing the pan

Crust
¹/₂ cup sesame seeds
1 cup graham cracker crumbs
2 tablespoons sugar
6 tablespoons unsalted butter, melted

Cake Batter
³/₄ cup (4 ounces) dried sour cherries
1¹/₂ pounds cream cheese, at room temperature
6 tablespoons unsalted butter, at room temperature
1 cup sugar
2 tablespoons cornstarch
4 large eggs, at room temperature
1 cup sour cream
1 tablespoon vanilla extract

1. Set a rack in the middle of the oven and preheat to 300°F. Grease the cake pan or springform with the melted butter.

2. THE CRUST: Toast the sesame seeds in a dry skillet over moderate heat, shaking the pan and tossing the seeds until lightly browned.

3. Combine the graham cracker crumbs, sugar, and sesame seeds in a medium bowl. Add the melted butter and mix well. Pat the mixture gently and evenly over the bottom of the prepared pan.

4. THE BATTER: Combine the cherries and 1 cup water in a small saucepan and bring to a boil over medium heat. Remove from the heat and set aside.

5. Put the cream cheese, butter, sugar, and cornstarch in a mixing bowl and beat at medium speed just to blend; take care not to beat too much air into the batter. Add the eggs one at a time, beating until each is incorporated. Reduce the speed and beat in the sour cream and vanilla. Drain the cherries, add them to the batter, and beat just to distribute them evenly.

6. Pour the batter into the prepared pan. Set the pan in a larger pan, such as a roasting pan, and pour about an inch of hot water into the larger pan. Bake for 1 hour and 15 minutes to $1^{1}/_{2}$ hours, or until lightly tanned, slightly puffy, and firm. Cool to room temperature in the water bath. Then remove from the water bath and refrigerate overnight.

7. Remove the cake from the pan, following the instructions on page 31.

Makes one 8-inch cake
Store for up to 4 days, wrapped, in the refrigerator.

PIES AND TARTS

Pie Fight at the O.K. Corral

Sitting on the Continental Divide in New Mexico is a municipality that is actually called Pie Town. From Josie's in Santa Fe to The Paris Coffee Shop in Fort Worth, everyone loves pies. They're not as easy as they look, but, if you follow the rules, they're a lot easier than you might think.

1. Keep all the ingredients cold, especially the shortening, and keep the dough chilled too. Time and cold are your best friends. They hinder protein formation (rubbery dough) and help lamination (flaky dough). Cold shortening smears between flour in layers, making flakes. Warm shortening soaks in and makes cardboard. In warm weather, work in the morning, before things heat up. When in doubt, throw your dough back in the refrigerator until it firms up a bit.

2. To test dough, pick up a fistful and squeeze it into a ball. If it just holds together, it is ready. Small chunks of butter remaining in the dough are fine.

3. For easy rolling, lightly dust your rolling pin and work surface with flour. Still having trouble? Roll between two sheets of waxed paper.

4. If your dough ends up thicker in the middle, try stopping your rolling pin before it goes over the edge. Each stroke should go only in one direction. Roll, don't scratch or scrunch the dough.

5. Dried beans make great pie weights. I've been using the same beans for over four years.

6. Patch holes in a raw shell by gluing on scraps of dough with a little water. If holes develop in shells as they bake, stick your dough patches on with a few drops of mucilage made by mixing an egg with two tablespoons of water.

7. If your top crust is browning too quickly, set a foil tent over it, or place a cookie sheet on an oven rack right above it.

8. You can make any of the pie or tart doughs in this book in a stand mixer; just be careful not to overblend.

9. Cleaning up a messy oven is never fun, so place a cookie sheet under your pie or tart. It will catch the drips and help distribute the heat evenly.

Mango
Meringue
Pie

(page 45)

*Linzer
Hearts
of the
West*

(page 144)

Espresso-Mascarpone Quesadillas with Mixed Fruit (page 112)

Clockwise from left: Petrified Forest Chocolate Cake (page 19);
Lemon-Lime Natilla (page 94) *and chocolate pudding with Chocolate
Hazelnut Crackers* (page 143); *Mexican Gold Nugget Brownie Torte*
(page 23); *Texas Pink Grapefruit, Tequila, and Burnt Orange Ices*
(pages 173, 172, 171); *Chocolate Custard Corn Pone* (page 102) *with
Chocolate Piki Bread* (page 106); *Chocolate-Raspberry Crisp* (page 71)

*From top:
Peanut
Butter Fudge
Ice Cream
(page 156)
on Peanut
Oatmeal Cook
(page 126),
Fresh Corn I
Cream (page
150)
on Molettes
(page 128), an
Sweet Potato
Ice Cream
(page 165)
on pistachio
fudge cookie*

Papaya Upside-Down Cake

(page 7)

Lemon Coconut Tart

The yummiest coconut macaroons in the universe are from the Casa Fresen Bakery in Arroyo Seco, New Mexico. They are the inspiration for this lemon curd tart. A coconut batter is molded against the sides of the tart tin and baked to form a chewy wall of meringue crust. Do try to find unsweetened coconut. It is available in specialty shops, health food stores, and some Southeast Asian groceries.

Coconut Tart Shell	Lemon Curd
$3/4$ cup all-purpose flour	2 tablespoons cornstarch
1 tablespoon sugar	$1/2$ cup heavy cream
$2^{1}/4$ cups unsweetened	2 large eggs
shredded coconut	4 large egg yolks
5 tablespoons cold unsalted	Grated zest of 1 lemon
butter, cut into pea-sized bits	$3/4$ cup fresh lemon juice
1 large egg lightly beaten with	(4 to 5 lemons)
1 cup ice water	$1/2$ cup fresh orange juice
2 large egg whites	4 tablespoons unsalted butter
1 cup confectioners' sugar	1 teaspoon vanilla extract
1 teaspoon vanilla extract	$3/4$ cup sugar

1. THE TART SHELL: In a large bowl, stir the flour, sugar, and $1/4$ cup of the coconut together. Using a pastry blender or your fingertips, work the butter into the mixture until it resembles coarse meal. Sprinkle on 2 to 3 tablespoons of the eggy water and mix it in with your fingers just until the dough comes together into a ball. Working on a lightly floured surface, take egg-sized pieces of the dough

and smear them away from you with the heel of your hand into 6-inch streaks. Scrape up all the streaks of dough and pile them on top of one another to form a disk. Wrap in plastic and refrigerate for at least 2 hours, or overnight.

2. Set a rack in the middle of the oven and preheat to 400°F. Lightly butter a $9^1/_2$-inch tart pan with a removable bottom.

3. On a lightly floured surface, roll the dough into a $9^1/_2$-inch circle. (For a perfect $9^1/_2$-inch circle of dough, use the rim of the tart pan as a giant cookie cutter.) Fit the dough into the bottom of the tart pan. Prick the dough all over with a fork.

4. In a medium bowl, mix the remaining 2 cups coconut, the egg whites, confectioners' sugar, and vanilla together. Lightly press this macaroon mixture against the sides of the tart pan to form the wall of the tart.

5. Bake the shell for 25 minutes, or until the bottom crust is tanned and the sides are golden brown. Let cool on a rack.

6. THE LEMON CURD: In a medium bowl, whisk the cornstarch and cream together until smooth. Then whisk in the eggs and yolks.

7. In a medium saucepan, combine the lemon zest, juices, butter, vanilla, and sugar and bring to a boil over medium heat. Whisking constantly, slowly drizzle half of the hot liquid into the cream mixture. Return the mixture to the saucepan and cook, whisking constantly and scraping the bottom of the pan, until tiny bubbles boil up for 10 seconds.

8. Strain the curd through a fine-mesh sieve into the tart shell. Let cool for 1 hour, then remove from the pan and refrigerate until chilled and set.

Makes one $9^1/_2$-inch tart
Store for up to 2 days in the refrigerator.

Chocolate-Crusted Tangerine Pie

The chocolate crust for this tangerine curd pie has a crunchy, cookie texture, and it is fine to make it in a food processor. You can bake it in a nine-and-a-half-inch tart pan if you prefer, but you will need to use foil and weights to hold up the sides during baking.

Chocolate Pie Shell

1½ cups all-purpose flour

¼ cup sugar

2 tablespoons unsweetened cocoa powder

8 tablespoons (1 stick) unsalted butter, at room temperature

1 large egg

Tangerine Curd

2 tablespoons cornstarch

¼ cup heavy cream

2 large eggs

4 large egg yolks

Grated zest of 2 tangerines

1½ cups fresh tangerine juice (8 to 9 tangerines)

4 tablespoons unsalted butter, cut into pieces

½ cup sugar

1. THE CHOCOLATE SHELL: Put the flour, sugar, and cocoa into the bowl of a food processor fitted with the metal blade. Pulsing the machine, add the butter bit by bit. Add the egg and process until the dough is thoroughly blended and masses together. Shape the dough into a disk.

2. Roll the dough out between 2 sheets of wax paper into a 12-inch circle about ⅛

inch thick. Peel off the top sheet of wax paper and invert the dough circle into a 9-inch pie plate. Peel off the second sheet of wax paper. Fold the overhanging dough under itself and crimp it against the rim of the plate with a fork. Prick the bottom all over with a fork and freeze for 30 minutes.

3. Set a rack in the middle of the oven and preheat to 400°F.

4. Bake the pie shell for 15 minutes, until just golden. Transfer to a rack to cool.

5. THE TANGERINE CURD: In a medium bowl, whisk the cornstarch and cream together until smooth. Whisk in the eggs and yolks.

6. In a medium nonreactive saucepan, combine the tangerine zest, juice, butter, and sugar and bring to a boil over medium heat. Whisking constantly, slowly drizzle half of the hot liquid into the cream mixture. Return the mixture to the saucepan and cook, whisking constantly and scraping the bottom of the pan, until tiny bubbles boil up for 10 seconds.

7. Strain the curd through a fine-mesh strainer into the chocolate pie shell. Let cool for 1 hour, then refrigerate until chilled and set.

Makes one 9¹/₂-inch pie
Store for up to 2 days in the refrigerator.

Note: You may also make this dough in a standing mixer or by hand.

Mango Meringue Pie

Tangy, creamy mango makes a distinctly flavorful alternative to traditional lemon in this meringue pie. Beating the egg whites until they are as warm as bathtub water makes a more durable meringue that won't "weep." The pie crust acts as a hitching post, so anchor the meringue up against it, or you are liable to have a topping that will mosey on down across the mango surface.

Flaky Pie Dough

3 tablespoons solid vegetable
   shortening
1^1/$_2$ cups all-purpose flour
2 teaspoons sugar
8 tablespoons (1 stick) cold
   unsalted butter, cut into pea-
   sized bits
3 to 4 tablespoons ice water

Mango Curd

2 tablespoons cornstarch
2 tablespoons fresh lemon juice

^{3}/$_4$ cup water
2 large eggs
4 large egg yolks
3 ripe mangoes, peeled and
   sliced (see Note, page 164)
4 tablespoons unsalted butter
^{1}/$_2$ cup sugar

Meringue

5 large egg whites
^{1}/$_2$ cup sugar
^{1}/$_4$ teaspoon salt
Pinch of cream of tartar

1. THE DOUGH: Flatten the shortening between 2 sheets of wax paper to a thickness of ^{1}/$_8$ inch. Remove the top sheet and, with a butter knife, draw a crisscross pattern through the shortening to divide it into ^{1}/$_2$-inch squares. Freeze for at least 30 minutes.

continued

2. In a large bowl, stir the flour and sugar together. Using a pastry blender or your fingertips, work the butter into the mixture until it resembles coarse meal. Quickly mix in the shortening squares. Sprinkle on the ice water and mix it in with your fingers just until the dough comes together into a ball. Wrap in plastic and refrigerate for at least 2 hours, or overnight.

3. On a lightly floured surface, roll the dough into a 12-inch circle about $1/8$ inch thick. Fit it into a 9-inch pie plate. Fold the overhanging dough under itself and decoratively crimp it against the rim of the plate. Prick the bottom all over with a fork. Freeze for 30 minutes.

4. Set a rack in the middle of the oven and preheat to 400°F.

5. Line the pie shell with aluminum foil and weight down with dried beans or pie weights. Bake for 20 minutes. Remove the foil and weights, and bake for 8 minutes longer, or until very lightly browned. Transfer to a wire rack to cool.

6. THE MANGO CURD: In a medium bowl, whisk the cornstarch, lemon juice, and $1/4$ cup of the water together until smooth. Whisk in the eggs and yolks.

7. Puree the mangoes with the remaining $1/2$ cup water in a food processor fitted with the metal blade.

8. In a medium nonreactive saucepan, combine the mango puree, butter, and sugar and bring to a boil over medium heat. Whisking constantly, slowly drizzle half of the hot liquid into the cornstarch mixture. Return the mixture to the saucepan and cook, whisking constantly and scraping the bottom of the pan, until tiny bubbles boil up for 10 seconds.

9. Strain the curd through a fine-mesh sieve into the pie shell. Let cool for 1 hour, then refrigerate until chilled and set.

10. THE MERINGUE: Combine the egg whites, sugar, salt, and cream of tartar in a large dry bowl and set it over a saucepan of simmering water. Whisk constantly until the mixture is lukewarm. Remove from the heat and continue to whisk (you can switch to an electric mixer) until the egg whites hold stiff peaks.

11. With the back of a spoon, spread the meringue on the top of the pie, making sure that the meringue touches the crust all around. Pull up wisps of meringue with the spoon as you go. Set the pie under a preheated broiler for 20 seconds, or pass the flame of a propane torch over the meringue, until lightly browned in spots.

Makes one 9-inch pie
Store for up to 24 hours in the refrigerator,
but best served the same day.

Chocolate Graham Pie

This chocolate truffle pie is rich and packed with a blast of dried fruit flavor. All you need is a thin slice and a glob of whipped cream.

1 tablespoon unsalted butter, melted, for greasing the pan

Graham Crust

2 cups graham cracker crumbs
1/4 cup sugar
10 tablespoons unsalted butter, melted

Chocolate Filling

1 cup shelled pumpkin seeds

6 ounces semisweet chocolate, coarsely chopped
3/4 cup heavy cream
1/4 cup Kahlúa
1 cup dried fruit (raisins, apricots, prunes, apples, currants, cranberries, and/or cherries in any combination), cut into bite-sized chunks

1. Set one rack in the bottom third of the oven and another in the top third, and preheat to 350°F. Grease a 9-inch pie pan with the melted butter.
2. THE CRUST: Mix the graham cracker crumbs and sugar in a medium bowl. Add the melted butter and mix well. Pat the mixture gently and evenly over the bottom of the prepared pie pan and up the sides. Chill for 15 minutes.
3. Meanwhile, spread the pumpkin seeds for the filling on a cookie sheet and toast on the top rack of the oven for 5 minutes, or until you hear them pop for 2 minutes. Turn the pan once for even toasting. Let cool.

4. Bake the graham crust on the bottom rack of the oven for 15 minutes, until dry and solid. Transfer to a rack to cool.

5. THE FILLING: Put the chocolate in a medium bowl. In a small saucepan, bring the cream and Kahlúa to a scald over medium heat. Pour the hot liquid over the chocolate, and gently stir to melt and blend until smooth. Fold in the dried fruit.

6. Taking care not to disturb the crust, pour the filling into the pie shell. Sprinkle the pumpkin seeds on top. Refrigerate for at least 2 hours, until set.

Makes one 9-inch pie
Store for 3 to 5 days in the refrigerator.

Cashew Tart

This nut tart is a lot like its clear-custard cousins, pecan and shoofly pies. Handle it gently—don't overcook or overheat—and you won't end up with a curdled mess. Leaks are the worst enemies of clear custards, so be sure to patch up any holes that develop in the shell. As a further precaution, I like to prebake the shell and glaze it watertight with a flour-enforced egg wash. You can use any dark rum in the filling, but, believe me, Jamaican rum, such as Myers's or Appleton's, is the stuff you really want.

Melted butter or nonstick spray
for greasing the pan

Tart Dough

1¹/₂ cups all-purpose flour
1 tablespoon plus 1 teaspoon
sugar
8 tablespoons (1 stick) cold
unsalted butter, cut into pea-
sized bits
1 large egg beaten with 1 cup
ice water

Egg Wash

2 tablespoons water
1 tablespoon all-purpose flour
1 large egg yolk

Cashew Filling

³/₄ cup sugar
4 large eggs
1 cup dark corn syrup
2 tablespoons Myers's or other
dark rum
1 tablespoon vanilla extract
4 tablespoons unsalted butter,
melted
2 cups (10 ounces) roasted
unsalted cashews

1. THE DOUGH: In a large bowl, stir the flour and sugar together. Using a pastry blender or your fingertips, work the butter into the mixture until it resembles coarse meal. Sprinkle on 3 to 4 tablespoons of the eggy water, and mix it in with your fingers just until the dough comes together into a ball. Working on a lightly floured surface, take egg-sized pieces of the dough and smear them away from you with the heel of your hand into 6-inch streaks. Scrape up all the streaks of dough and pile them on top of one another to form a disk. Wrap in plastic and refrigerate for at least 2 hours, or overnight.

2. Set a rack in the middle of the oven and preheat to 400°F. Lightly butter a 9^1/$_2$-inch tart pan with a removable bottom.

3. With a fork, mix together the water, flour, and egg yolk in a small bowl to make an egg wash. Cover and refrigerate.

4. On a lightly floured surface, roll the dough into an 11^1/$_2$-inch circle. Fit the dough into the prepared pan. Trim the excess dough to a 1-inch overhang, and double the dough over itself to reinforce the sides. (Save the trimmings for any emergency patchwork.) Refrigerate for 20 minutes.

5. Line the tart shell with aluminum foil and weight down with dried beans or pie weights. Bake for 20 minutes. Remove the foil and bake for 5 minutes longer, or until lightly browned. Patch any visible holes in the shell with the reserved dough scraps. Paint the shell with the egg wash, and return to the oven for 5 more minutes, until the wash is shiny and no longer runny. Transfer to a rack, and lower the oven temperature to 325°F.

6. THE FILLING: In a large bowl, lightly beat the sugar and eggs together. Add the corn syrup, rum, and vanilla and beat just to blend. Mix in the melted butter.

7. Spread the cashews in the partially baked shell and cover with the filling, mak-

ing sure all the nuts are covered. Bake for 30 minutes, or until little bubbles appear around the edges of the tart and the center looks barely set. Transfer to a rack to cool.

Makes one 9¹/₂-inch tart
Store for up to 3 days at room temperature.

Apple-Raspberry Pie

Summer ends and fall begins with an overlapping of the raspberry and apple harvests. The mellow tartness of balsamic vinegar helps to tie the two fruits together in this two-crusted pie. Instead of painting the entire crust with egg wash, I just dab it on in spots, so it browns unevenly and looks like the coat of a pinto pony.

Double-Crust Pie Dough

1/4 cup plus 2 tablespoons solid
   vegetable shortening
3 cups all-purpose flour
8 ounces (2 sticks) cold
   unsalted butter, cut into pea-
   sized bits
2 to 3 tablespoons ice water

Apple-Raspberry Filling

2 1/2 pounds baking apples,
   such as Granny Smith,
   Rome, Golden Delicious, or
   McIntosh, cut into eighths
1/4 cup sugar
1/4 cup cornstarch
1/4 teaspoon cinnamon
1 tablespoon balsamic vinegar
1/2 pint raspberries

1 large egg white beaten with
   2 tablespoons water for
   egg wash
1 tablespoon sugar

1. THE DOUGH: Flatten the shortening between 2 sheets of wax paper to a thickness of 1/8 inch. With a butter knife, draw a crisscross pattern through the shortening to divide it into 1/2-inch squares. Freeze for at least 30 minutes.

continued

2. Put the flour in a large bowl. Using a pastry blender or your fingertips, work in the butter until the mixture resembles coarse meal. Quickly mix in the shortening squares. Gradually sprinkle on the ice water and mix it in with your fingers just until the dough comes together into a ball. Divide the dough in half and pat into two ³/₄-inch-thick disks. Wrap in plastic wrap and refrigerate for at least 2 hours, or overnight.

3. Set a rack in the middle of the oven and preheat to 400°F.

4. THE FILLING: In a medium bowl, combine the apple chunks, sugar, cornstarch, cinnamon, and vinegar and toss to mix. Gently stir in the raspberries.

5. On a lightly floured surface, roll out one disk of dough into a 12-inch circle about ¹/₈ inch thick. Fit the circle into a 9-inch pie plate. Pile the apple filling into the pie pan.

6. Roll out the remaining disk of dough to a 12-inch circle. Lightly moisten the edges of the bottom crust, and drape the second circle of dough on top. Press the edges of the dough together and trim to a 1-inch overhang. Tuck the overhanging dough under itself and pinch together to form a decorative edge.

7. With a pastry brush, paint a light, uneven coating of egg wash over the crust, then sprinkle on the sugar. With scissors, cut 5 steam vents in the crust.

8. Bake for 35 minutes. Reduce the oven temperature to 350°F and bake for 25 minutes longer or until the top crust is brown and the filling is bubbling. Transfer to a rack to cool.

Makes one 9-inch pie
Store for up to 2 days at room temperature.

Sour Cream Custard-Pear Pie

There's lots of talk about comfort foods. They aren't highfalutin, but homey, home on the range stuff that leaves you satisfied. A slice (or, more accurately, hunk) of this pie doesn't fool around: pears in a sour cream custard filling, covered with crumbly cinnamon streusel, and baked in a spiced crust.

Sugar and Spice Pie Dough

3 tablespoons solid vegetable shortening

8 tablespoons (1 stick) cold unsalted butter, cut into pea-sized bits

1½ cups all-purpose flour

2 tablespoons sugar

½ teaspoon cinnamon

¼ teaspoon ground cloves

3 to 4 tablespoons ice water

Cinnamon Streusel

1 cup all-purpose flour

1¼ cup lightly packed light brown sugar

1 teaspoon cinnamon

4 tablespoons cold unsalted butter, cut into pea-sized bits

Sour Cream Pear Filling

¼ cup sugar

2 tablespoons all-purpose flour

continued

¹/₂ *cup sour cream*
2 teaspoons vanilla extract
1 large egg
2 large egg yolks

4 Bartlett or Bosc pears,
   peeled, halved, cored, and
   cut into lengthwise ¹/₄-inch
   slices

1. THE DOUGH: Flatten the shortening between 2 sheets of wax paper, to a thickness of $1/8$ inch. Peel off the top sheet and, with a butter knife, draw a crisscross pattern through the shortening to divide it into $1/2$-inch squares. Freeze for at least 30 minutes.

2. In a large bowl, stir the flour, sugar, cinnamon, and cloves together. Using a pastry blender or your fingertips, work in the butter until the mixture resembles coarse meal. Quickly mix in the shortening squares. Gradually sprinkle on the ice water and mix it in with your fingers just until the dough comes together into a ball. Pat into a $3/4$-inch-thick disk, wrap in plastic wrap, and refrigerate for at least 2 hours, or overnight.

3. Set a rack in the middle of the oven and preheat to 400°F.

4. On a lightly floured surface, roll the dough into a 12-inch circle about $1/8$ inch thick. Fit it into a 9-inch pie plate. Trim, then fold the overhanging dough under itself and decoratively crimp it against the rim of the plate. Prick the dough all over with a fork. Freeze for 20 minutes.

5. Line the pie shell with aluminum foil and weight down with dried beans or pie weights. Bake for 12 minutes. Remove the foil and bake for 5 minutes longer, or until the pastry looks dry. Transfer to a wire rack, and lower the oven temperature to 325°F.

6. Meanwhile, make the streusel: Combine the flour, brown sugar, and cinnamon in a medium bowl. Work in the butter, rubbing and pinching it between your fingers until the mixture looks mealy and lumpy. Don't overwork to the point that it becomes sticky. Set aside.

7. THE FILLING: In a medium bowl, whisk the sugar and flour together. Blend in the sour cream, vanilla, and then the egg and yolks. Fold in the pear slices.

8. Scrape the filling into the partially baked pie shell and sprinkle the streusel evenly over the top. Bake for 45 minutes, or until the custard is set. Transfer to a rack to cool.

Makes one 9-inch pie
Store for up to 2 days in the refrigerator.

Note: Although Bartlett or Bosc are preferable, in a pinch you can use D'Anjou pears. Never bake with Comice, which will fall apart.

Cornmeal-Crusted Apple Tart

With good old American ingenuity, and crunchy cornmeal, the classic French apple tart attains yummy new heights. The most difficult thing about making this tart is slicing the apples thin enough. In restaurants, a gadget called a mandoline is used to produce skinny, uniform slices. If a knife is all you have, then just do your best. If the slices are a bit uneven, they will still bake all gooey, golden, and caramelized.

Cornmeal Tart Dough

1 cup all-purpose flour

3 tablespoons yellow cornmeal

1 tablespoon sugar

6 tablespoons cold unsalted butter, cut into pea-sized bits

1 large egg, beaten with 1 cup ice water

Caramelized Apple Topping

6 medium baking apples, such as Granny Smith, Rome, McIntosh, or Golden Delicious, peeled, cored, and sliced crosswise into $1/16$-inch-thick rounds

6 tablespoons unsalted butter, melted

$1/2$ cup confectioners' sugar

$1/4$ cup granulated sugar

1 teaspoon cinnamon

1. THE DOUGH: In a large bowl, stir together the flour, cornmeal, and sugar with a whisk. Using a pastry blender or your fingertips, work in the butter until the mixture resembles coarse meal. Sprinkle on 2 to 3 tablespoons of the eggy water and mix it in with your fingers just until the dough comes together into a ball. Working on a lightly floured surface, take egg-sized pieces of the dough and

smear them away from you with the heel of your hand into 6-inch streaks. Scrape up all the streaks of dough and pile them on top of one another to form a disk. Wrap in plastic wrap and refrigerate for at least 2 hours, or overnight.

2. On a lightly floured surface, roll the dough into a circle slightly larger than 10 inches in diameter and about $1/4$ inch thick. Using a 10-inch plate as a guide, trim with a sharp knife to a 10-inch round. Transfer to a parchment paper–lined or non-stick cookie sheet and refrigerate for 1 hour.

3. Set a rack in the middle of the oven and preheat to 400°F.

4. Using the largest apple slices, arrange them in a ring $1/4$ inch from the edge of the dough round, overlapping them by about $3/8$ inch. Arrange another ring of slices $1^1/2$ inches from the edge, overlapping the first ring. Using the smallest slices, arrange a final ring in the center of the tart. Fill in any empty space in the center with leftover scraps.

5. With a pastry brush, lightly coat the tart with about 2 tablespoons of the melted butter. Mix the confectioners' sugar, granulated sugar, and cinnamon in a small bowl. Sprinkle $1/4$ cup of the sugar mixture evenly over the tart; for best results, tap it through a small strainer.

6. Bake the tart for 10 minutes, then remove from the oven. Sprinkle another $1/4$ cup of the sugar mixture over the tart, and brush with melted butter. Bake for 10 more minutes, and repeat the process with the remaining sugar mixture and butter. Bake for 10 minutes longer, or until the tart bottom is lightly browned. Transfer to a wire rack to cool.

Makes one 10-inch tart
This tart is best eaten the same day.

Note: You may make six individual 4-inch tarts with this recipe. Use smaller apples so the slices will overlap easily.

Sweet Potato Tart

Texas starts in the Deep South and ends up in the golden West. With hundreds of miles of Mexican border and an ethnically diverse population, you've got yourself quite a culinary heritage. Pureed sweet potatoes spiced with cinnamon and cloves are a traditional Southern pie filling, but the combination also works wonderfully when the potatoes are sliced and baked on a flat tart shell. Try to find long, thin sweet potatoes; they are easier to slice.

1 recipe Cornmeal Tart Dough
  (page 58), rolled into a
  10-inch circle (see page 59),
  placed on a parchment
  paper–lined or nonstick
  baking sheet, and chilled
2 pounds sweet potatoes,
  peeled and sliced crosswise
  1/8 inch thick

6 tablespoons unsalted butter,
  melted
1/2 cup confectioners' sugar
1/4 cup granulated sugar
1 teaspoon cinnamon
1/2 teaspoon ground cloves

1. Set a rack in the middle of the oven and preheat to 400°F.
2. Using the largest sweet potato slices, arrange them in a ring 1/4 inch from the edge of the dough round, overlapping them by about 1/2 inch. Arrange another ring of slices 1 1/2 inches from the edge, overlapping the first ring. Using the smallest slices, arrange a final ring in the center of the tart. Fill in any empty space in the center with leftover scraps.

3. With a pastry brush, lightly coat the tart with melted butter. Mix the confectioners' sugar, granulated sugar, cinnamon, and cloves in a small bowl. Sprinkle $1/4$ cup of the sugar mixture evenly over the tart; for best results, tap it through a small strainer.

4. Bake the tart for 10 minutes, then remove from the oven, sprinkle another $1/4$ cup of the sugar mixture over the tart, and brush with melted butter. Bake for 10 more minutes, and repeat the process with the remaining sugar mixture and butter. Bake for 10 minutes longer, or until the tart bottom is lightly browned. Cool the tart on a wire rack.

Makes one 10-inch tart
Store for up to 2 days at room temperature.

Note: You may make six individual 4-inch tarts with this recipe. Use slender sweet potatoes so the slices will overlap easily.

COBBLERS, CRISPS, AND SHORTCAKES

Bow and Arrowroot

"As easy as pie." Now, who said that? The bottom crust gets soggy while the top gets burned, the sides cave in, the crust collapses, and the filling runs all over the place. "As problematic as pie"—now that's a proverb.

Cobblers, crisps, and pandowdies are easy. They are pies without bottoms or sides, sort of like sweet casseroles. In some cases you can even bake the crust separately, ensuring a perfect product. Serve them warm with ice cream or vanilla custard.

Rhubarb Crisp with Anise Streusel

A lot of people are afraid of rhubarb, not because parts of it (the green leaves) are poisonous, but because they just don't know what to do with the stuff. Well, it's not really so dangerous, and it's a whole lot easier to handle than you might think.

Always cut off all the rhubarb leaves and discard them. Green parts of the remaining stalks are fine, but the redder the rhubarb, the tastier. Don't bother with peeling, as you'll waste the best part. Just wash well to release any clinging soil.

Anise is a wonderful flavor for a crumb streusel topping; it complements the sweet-tart rhubarb perfectly. Serve this crisp warm, with Brown Sugar–Vanilla Ice Cream (page 160) or Vanilla Custard Sauce (page 194).

1 bunch rhubarb, cut into
¹/₂-inch chunks (about
4¹/₂ cups)
¹/₂ cup sugar

Anise Streusel
2 cups all-purpose flour
¹/₂ cup lightly packed brown
sugar

1 tablespoon ground anise
(see Note)
8 tablespoons (1 stick) cold
unsalted butter, cut into
pea-sized bits

1 teaspoon cornstarch
¹/₄ cup fresh orange juice
1 teaspoon fresh lemon juice

1. Put the rhubarb in a large bowl and sprinkle it with the sugar. Let it sit for 1 hour to exude, or "sweat" out, some of its juices.

2. THE STREUSEL: Combine the flour, brown sugar, and anise in a medium bowl. Work in the butter, rubbing and pinching it with your fingers until the mixture looks mealy and lumpy. Don't overwork to the point that it becomes sticky.

3. Set a rack in the middle of the oven and preheat to 375°F.

4. In a small bowl, whisk the cornstarch with the orange and lemon juices until smooth. Let sit for 1 minute, then whisk again and stir into the macerating rhubarb. Transfer to a shallow 2-quart baking dish.

5. Sprinkle the streusel evenly over the rhubarb. Bake for 40 minutes, or until golden brown on top and bubbly.

Serves 6 to 8

Note: If you can't find ground anise, grind star anise in a coffee mill —this is the way I do it.

Caramel Pear Pandowdy

If you have been thrifty and saved scraps of pie or tart dough in your freezer, you will have a head start on this pandowdy. If you have thrown caution and dough scraps to the wind, you can always make a new batch. To dowdy something (from Ye Olde English) means to cut its crust up and dunk it into the goop underneath. Don't try to be neat with the servings—just dig right in with a big spoon.

4 tablespoons unsalted butter

¾ cup sugar

6 medium Bartlett or Bosc
pears, peeled, cored, and cut
lengthwise into 6 slices each

1 recipe Sugar and Spice Pie
Dough (page 55), or scraps
of tart or pie dough, rolled
into a 9-inch round and
chilled

1. Set a rack in the middle of the oven and preheat to 375°F.

2. In a 9-inch ovenproof skillet, melt the butter and sugar together over moderately high heat. Continue to cook the syrup until it turns a light caramel color, swirling the pan as necessary for even coloring. Remove from the heat.

3. Arrange the pear slices in tight concentric circles in the skillet. If you have enough extra pear slices, distribute them evenly in a second layer. Cook over moderate heat for 10 minutes, then remove from the heat.

4. Prick a few holes in the dough with a fork, and lay it over the pears. Bake the pandowdy for 20 minutes, or until the crust is golden brown and cooked through. Be careful: Both the pan and the filling will be very hot. Let cool for 5 minutes before serving.

Serves 6 to 8

Black Friar Plum Buckle

Buckles, or slumps as they are called in some parts of the country, are half cake and half cobbler—fruit on the bottom and cake on the top. Sweet, tart, and juicy. Black Friar plums work great, but don't be afraid to try Santa Rosa or even green Kelsey.

Plum Filling

3 tablespoons cornstarch

1 cup Japanese plum wine
   (see Note) or port

1 cup sugar

2 pounds ripe Black Friar
   plums, pitted and cut into
   6 wedges each

Cake

3/4 cup cake flour

1/2 teaspoon baking powder

1/4 teaspoon baking soda

Pinch of salt

*4 tablespoons unsalted butter,
   at room temperature*

1/2 cup sugar

*1 large egg, at room
   temperature*

1 teaspoon vanilla extract

*1/4 cup plus 2 tablespoons
   buttermilk, at room
   temperature*

1. Set a rack in the middle of the oven and preheat to 375°F.
2. In a medium saucepan, whisk the cornstarch into the plum wine. Add the sugar and bring to a boil, whisking over medium heat. Boil for 2 to 3 minutes to evaporate some of the alcohol and thicken. Remove from the heat.
3. Place the plums in a shallow 2-quart baking dish. Stir in the plum wine mixture.

continued

4. Sift the flour, baking powder, baking soda, and salt together onto a sheet of waxed paper. Sift 2 more times to mix and aerate.

5. Put the butter and sugar in the bowl of an electric mixer and beat at high speed for 30 seconds, until well blended and smooth. Add the egg and beat, scraping down the sides of the bowl, if necessary, until light and fluffy, about 5 more minutes. With the mixer on its lowest setting, or using a rubber spatula, beat or fold in one third of the flour mixture. Beat or fold in the vanilla and half of the buttermilk, and then another one third of the flour mixture. Beat or fold in the remaining buttermilk and the remaining flour mixture.

6. Spread the batter over the plums. Bake for 35 minutes, or until the cake is golden and the center springs back when lightly pressed. Serve warm.

Serves 8

Note: Japanese plum wine is available in better liquor stores.
I prefer Fuki.

Apple-Cranberry Crisp with Sunflower Seed Streusel

Sunflowers were the first crop grown in the Southwest. Not only were they a valuable food source but they were also used for ceremonial face paint and hair grooming. In this East-meets-West combination, tart New England cranberries complement a rich sunflower seed streusel topping.

Fruit

2 pounds baking apples, such
    as Granny Smith, Rome,
    Golden Delicious, or
    McIntosh, peeled, cored, and
    cut into 1/2-inch wedges

1 cup fresh or frozen unthawed
    cranberries

3/4 cup lightly packed dark
    brown sugar

1/4 cup applejack (see Notes)

1 tablespoon vanilla extract

Streusel Topping

1 cup all-purpose flour

1/2 cup sunflower seeds

1/2 cup lightly packed light
    brown sugar

1 teaspoon cinnamon

8 tablespoons (1 stick) cold
    unsalted butter, cut into
    pea-sized bits

1. Set a rack in the middle of the oven and preheat to 375°F. Lightly butter a shallow 2-quart baking dish.

2. THE FRUIT: In a medium bowl, toss the apples, cranberries, dark brown sugar, applejack, and vanilla together to mix well. Lightly pack the fruit mixture into the prepared baking dish.

3. THE STREUSEL: Combine the flour, sunflower seeds, light brown sugar, and cinnamon in a medium bowl. Work in the butter, rubbing and pinching it with your fingers until the mixture looks mealy and lumpy. Do not overwork to the point that it becomes sticky.

4. Sprinkle the streusel evenly over the fruit mixture. Bake for 40 minutes, or until golden brown on top and bubbly.

Serves 8

Notes: Applejack is an apple brandy with a nice, natural flavor; don't use any of those icky-flavored schnapps. However, an excellent and easy-to-find substitute is $1/4$ cup frozen apple juice concentrate.

Toasted pumpkin seeds would make a yummy substitution for the sunflower seeds—or use $1/4$ cup of each in the streusel.

Chocolate-Raspberry Crisp

Raspberries are delicate little creatures that can't put up with too long a spell in the heat. By separately prebaking the chocolate streusel, we shorten their stint in the oven. The berries are then covered with the crunchy crumb topping and warmed up in a pool of melted chocolate.

1 cup all-purpose flour
³/₄ cup cocoa
³/₄ cup sugar
5 ounces (1¹/₄ sticks) cold
   butter, cut into pea-sized bits

1¹/₂ pints raspberries
4 ounces semisweet chocolate,
   finely chopped

1. Set a rack in the middle of the oven and preheat to 375°F.
2. Combine the flour, cocoa, and sugar in a medium bowl. Work in the butter, rubbing and pinching it with your fingers until the mixture looks mealy and lumpy.
3. Distribute the streusel over a parchment-lined cookie sheet and bake for 10 minutes until set and dry on its surface. Set aside.
4. In a shallow 2-quart baking dish, gently mix the raspberries and chocolate together. Sprinkle on the streusel and bake for 7 minutes or until the chocolate has melted.

Serves 6 to 8

Blueberry Almond Shortcakes

For cowboys on the trail, biscuits were an essential part of every meal. Cooks lowered the tailgate of their chuck wagons to form a worktable. After mixing, kneading, and cutting the dough, they baked the biscuits in heavy Dutch ovens fitted with concave lids. Coals could be loaded into these lids so the "ovens" would be heated from top and bottom. These shortcakes are made from an old-fashioned cream biscuit recipe, jazzed up with toasted almonds.

Shortcakes

1¾ cups cake flour
¼ cup sugar
2 teaspoons baking powder
½ teaspoon salt
½ cup toasted sliced almonds
  (see page xxi)
8 tablespoons (1 stick) cold
  butter, cut into pea-sized bits

1 cup heavy cream
1 teaspoon vanilla extract
½ teaspoon almond extract

1 recipe Blueberry Sauce
  (page 192)
1 pint blueberries
1 recipe Whipped Cream
  (page 199)

1. THE SHORTCAKES: In a large bowl, stir together the flour, sugar, baking powder, and salt with a whisk to blend. Stir in the almonds. Using a pastry blender or your fingertips, work in the butter until the mixture resembles coarse meal. Add the cream and vanilla and almond extracts, and mix with a large spoon or fork to form a soft dough. Shape the dough into a ball and gently knead for about 30 seconds. Do not overwork.

2. On a lightly floured cookie sheet, pat or roll out the dough to a thickness of 1 inch. Refrigerate for at least 1 hour, to firm.

3. Set a rack in the middle of the oven and preheat to 375°F.

4. With a $2^{1}\!/_{2}$-inch round cutter, cut out biscuits from the chilled dough, and arrange them 2 inches apart on an ungreased cookie sheet. Gently pat the scraps together, chill for 15 minutes, and cut more biscuits. Repeat with any remaining scraps, if necessary, to make a total of 8 biscuits.

5. Bake the biscuits for 20 minutes, or until slightly tanned and the centers spring back when lightly pressed. Cool in the pan on a wire rack.

6. With a serrated knife, split the biscuits in half. Place the bottom halves on individual plates, and distribute the sauce, berries, and whipped cream over them. Save a dollop of whipped cream and a few berries as a garnish for the tippy top of each shortcake. Place the biscuit tops on top, and serve.

Serves 8

Chocolate Shortcakes with Chocolate Raspberry Salsa and Tia Maria Whipped Cream

Raspberries and chocolate are a match that can't be beat, so I've come up with a salsa that pairs them. Chocolate and a little chile pepper go pretty darn well, too. Put them together, and I think we've got ourselves a hootenanny.

Shortcakes

1½ cups cake flour

¼ cup sugar

¼ cup unsweetened cocoa
    powder

1 tablespoon plus 1 teaspoon
    baking powder

Pinch of salt

8 tablespoons (1 stick) cold
    unsalted butter, cut into pea-
    sized bits

1 cup heavy cream

Tia Maria Whipped Cream

1 cup heavy cream

1 tablespoon confectioners'
    sugar

1 tablespoon Tia Maria,
    Kahlúa, or other coffee-
    flavored liqueur

1 recipe Chocolate Raspberry
    Salsa (page 184)

Confectioners' sugar for
    dusting

1. THE SHORTCAKES: In a large bowl, stir together the flour, sugar, cocoa, baking powder, and salt with a whisk. Using a pastry blender or your fingertips, work in

the butter until the mixture resembles coarse meal. Add the cream and mix with a large spoon or fork to form a soft dough. Shape the dough into a ball and gently knead for about 30 seconds.

2. On a lightly floured cookie sheet, pat or roll out the dough to a thickness of 1 inch. Refrigerate for at least 1 hour, to firm.

3. Set a rack in the middle of the oven and preheat to 375°F.

4. With a 2^{1}/$_{2}$-inch round cutter, cut out biscuits from the chilled dough and space them 2 inches apart on an ungreased cookie sheet. Gently pat the scraps together, chill for 15 minutes, and cut more biscuits. Repeat with any remaining scraps if necessary, to make a total of 8 biscuits.

5. Bake the biscuits for 18 minutes, or until the centers spring back when lightly pressed. Cool in the pan on a wire rack.

6. THE WHIPPED CREAM: In a chilled bowl, whip the cream until thickened. Add the confectioners' sugar and Tia Maria, and beat until soft peaks form.

7. With a serrated knife, split the biscuits in half. Place the bottom halves on individual plates, and spoon the salsa and then the whipped cream over them. Place the biscuit tops on top, lightly dust with confectioners' sugar, and serve.

Serves 8

Note: Try these shortcakes with Strawberry-Almond Salsa (page 178), Raspberry-Cherimoya Chip Salsa (page 179), or Apricot-Hazelnut Salsa (page 182).

Pecan Fritters with Dried Fruit Stew

Traipsing around the peaks of northern New Mexico and southern Colorado, Kit Carson was the quintessential mountain man. His wife, however, had the somewhat dubious honor of having a stew of dried ingredients sort of named after her: the Bowl of the Wife of Kit Carson.

Here, crisp but cakey pecan fritters get dropped into a stew of dried fruits (a real mountain man staple). Serve with Vanilla Custard Sauce (page 194) on the side.

Fritters

1¹/₄ cups all-purpose flour

¹/₄ cup sugar

1 tablespoon baking powder

¹/₂ teaspoon salt

³/₄ cup coarsely chopped
   pecans

³/₄ cup water

¹/₂ cup cornmeal

¹/₂ cup buttermilk

1 large egg

1 teaspoon vanilla extract

Vegetable oil for deep-frying

Fruit Stew

2 cups white grape juice

¹/₄ cup sherry

2 teaspoons vanilla extract

2 cups dried fruit (raisins,
   apricots, prunes, apples,
   currants, cranberries, and/or
   cherries in any combination)

1 teaspoon cornstarch or
   arrowroot

Confectioners' sugar for
   dusting

1. Put the flour, sugar, baking powder, and salt in a medium bowl and stir together with a whisk. Stir in the pecans.

2. In a small saucepan, bring the water to a boil. Whisking constantly, gradually add the cornmeal. Continue to whisk and cook until the mush begins to sputter, then remove from the heat and stir in the buttermilk. Stir the mush into the flour mixture, then add the egg and vanilla and mix thoroughly. Let sit for 30 minutes.

3. Combine $1^{1}/_{2}$ cups of the grape juice, the sherry, and vanilla in a medium non-reactive saucepan. Add the dried fruit and bring to a simmer. In a small bowl, whisk the arrowroot or cornstarch and remaining $^{1}/_{2}$ cup grape juice together and stir into the fruit. Cook, stirring for 3 to 4 minutes, until thickened. Remove from the heat, and cover to keep warm.

4. In a deep-fryer or deep heavy saucepan, heat 2 inches of oil to 375°F (a drop of batter dropped into the oil will immediately bubble and sizzle). Working in batches, plop walnut-sized globs of the batter into the hot oil, and fry, turning once, until golden brown on both sides, 4 to 5 minutes. Drain on paper towels.

5. If necessary, reheat the fruit stew over low heat. To serve, divide the stew among serving bowls and top with 2 fritters, lightly dusted with confectioners' sugar.

Serves 6 to 8

Note: You can prepare the fritters and stew up to 8 hours in advance.
Reheat the stew on top of the stove. Reheat the fritters
in a 350°F oven for 8 minutes.

Peach Brown Betty

Summer pudding is the American descendant of the fancy European charlotte. Brown Betty is, in turn, summer pudding's funky country cousin, a roughshod but luscious casserole of juicy baked peaches and buttery brioche.

Melted butter for the dish
One ½-pound loaf brioche or
   challah bread, cut into
   pieces approximately 1 inch
   square
1½ pounds ripe peaches

¾ cup sugar
2 tablespoons vanilla extract
2 tablespoons framboise
  (see Note)
8 tablespoons (1 stick)
  unsalted butter, melted

1. One day in advance, spread the bread cubes out overnight on a cookie sheet to become stale, so they will be nice and absorbent. (You can also dry the bread in a 350°F oven. Spread on a baking sheet and toast, stirring occasionally, until lightly browned.)

2. Have ready a bowl of ice water. Plunge the peaches into boiling water for 1 minute, then transfer to the ice water; drain well. Slip the skins off and slice the peaches into ½-inch-thick wedges.

3. Put the peach slices, sugar, vanilla, and framboise in a medium bowl and toss well. Let macerate for 10 minutes.

4. Generously butter a shallow 2-quart baking dish.

5. Put the bread cubes in a large bowl and, while tossing, drizzle on the melted butter. Add the peach mixture and toss again. Pack the mixture into the pre-

pared baking dish. Cover the top with plastic wrap, and press down firmly to compress it. Refrigerate for at least 4 hours, or overnight.

6. Set a rack in the middle of the oven and preheat to 400°F.

7. Remove the plastic wrap, and bake the Betty for 35 minutes, or until lightly browned on top.

Serves 6 to 8

Note: Framboise, raspberry eau-de-vie, is available at better liquor stores.

CUSTARDS AND PUDDINGS

Straight Talk
About Custards and Flans

Trousers need suspenders, pies need pie plates, and custards need their crocks to hold them up. Flans, on the other hand, can be flipped out from their caramelized containers. Just like a tart, they will stand on their own.

Always play it safe and bake slowly. Flans and custards are not the kind of broncos that you want broken.

1. Heat the milk or cream just to the point of scalding (it will wiggle in the pot).

2. Add the hot liquid to the eggs gradually, or you may end up with a scrambled mess.

3. Whisk slowly, gently, and just enough to blend. You want to avoid air bubbles, which make custards coarse and grainy.

4. Fill the custard cups carefully, preferably by drizzling the custard down a spoon. This will leave anything you may have lined the cups with intact and prevent the formation of additional bubbles.

5. Custards have a way of showing just how unevenly our ovens heat. Check them often, and carefully turn the pan from front to back for even baking.

6. If you are uncertain about just when your custards or flans are done, opt for taking them out early. Let them cool down, covered, in their water bath. The slowpokes should firm up without overcooking the roadrunners.

Spanish Flan

Santa Fe was founded by the Spanish in 1610 (ten years before the Pilgrims landed on Plymouth Rock). With them, they brought watermelons, peaches, and, at some point, flan, the caramel-coated custard that is Spain's favorite dessert.

Caramel
1/4 cup water
1 cup sugar

Custard
1 1/2 cups milk
1 1/2 cups heavy cream

3/4 cup sugar
2 tablespoons cream sherry
    (such as Harvey's or Dry
    Sack)
4 large eggs
6 large egg yolks

1. THE CARAMEL: Put the water and sugar in a small heavy-bottomed saucepan, stir once and cook over high heat until the syrup turns a light amber color. Immediately divide the caramel syrup among 8 completely dry 6-ounce custard cups. Taking care not to touch the hot caramel, swirl the syrup to coat the bottoms and halfway up the sides of the cups.
2. Set a rack in the middle of the oven and preheat to 300°F.
3. THE CUSTARD: In a medium heavy-bottomed saucepan, combine the milk, cream, and 1 tablespoon of the sugar, and bring just to a scald.
4. Meanwhile, put the remaining sugar (1/2 cup plus 3 tablespoons), the sherry, eggs, and egg yolks in a large bowl and whisk just to blend.
5. While gently whisking the eggs, drizzle the hot cream mixture into them so that

they are gradually warmed up. Strain the custard into a pitcher, then pour it into the caramel-coated cups. Skim off any bubbles that have formed on the surface.

6. Put the cups in a roasting pan and add enough hot water to come halfway up the sides of the cups. Tightly cover the pan with foil. Bake for 45 to 55 minutes: The custards are ready when they still jiggle slightly when gently shaken but their surface is smooth and set. Let cool to room temperature in the water bath, then remove and refrigerate for at least 8 hours, or overnight.

7. To unmold, run a thin knife between the custard and the inside of each cup. Place a serving plate upside down over the cup and flip the whole thing over with a sharp shake. If the flan doesn't come right out, shake it a few more times. Serve immediately.

Makes 8 individual flans
Store for up to 3 days in the refrigerator.

Note: You can also make one large flan in a shallow five-cup baking dish. Increase the baking time by fifteen minutes.

Chocolate Flan

South of the border, flan takes all different forms, running the gamut from custards to cakelike puddings. What they all have in common is that they are baked in caramel-coated molds. This flan is a wiggly custard, richly flavored with chocolate. Make sure that your caramel is just a light amber color. Dark caramel has too sharp a flavor for chocolate.

Caramel
$^1/_4$ cup water
1 cup sugar

Custard
5 ounces semisweet chocolate,
  coarsely chopped

$1^1/_2$ cups milk
$1^1/_2$ cups heavy cream
$^1/_2$ cup sugar
3 large eggs
6 large egg yolks

1. THE CARAMEL: Put the water and sugar in a small heavy-bottomed saucepan. Stir once and cook over high heat until the syrup turns a light amber color. Immediately divide the caramel syrup among 8 completely dry 6-ounce custard cups. Taking care not to touch the hot caramel, swirl the syrup to coat the bottoms and halfway up the sides of the cups.
2. Set a rack in the middle of the oven and preheat to 300°F.
3. THE CUSTARD: Melt the chocolate in the top of a double boiler over barely simmering water or in a small dry bowl set over a saucepan of just-simmering water. Remove from the heat.

4. In a medium heavy-bottomed saucepan, combine the milk, cream, and 1 table-spoon of the sugar, and bring just to a scald.

5. Meanwhile, put the remaining sugar ($1/4$ cup plus 1 tablespoon), eggs, and egg yolks in a large bowl and whisk just to blend.

6. While gently whisking the eggs, drizzle the hot cream mixture into them so that they are gradually warmed up. Whisk in the warm chocolate. Strain the custard into a pitcher, then pour it into the caramel-coated cups. Skim off any bubbles that have formed on the surface.

7. Put the cups in a roasting pan and add enough hot water to come halfway up the sides of the cups. Tightly cover the pan with foil and bake for 45 to 55 minutes: The custards are ready when they still jiggle slightly when gently shaken but their surface is smooth and set. Let cool to room temperature in the water bath, then remove and refrigerate for at least 4 hours, or overnight.

8. To unmold, run a thin knife between the custard and the inside of each cup. Place a serving plate upside down over the cup and flip the whole thing over with a sharp shake. If the flan doesn't come right out, shake it a few more times. Serve immediately.

Makes 8 individual flans
Store for up to 3 days in the refrigerator.

Note: You can also make one large flan in a shallow five-cup baking dish. Increase the baking time by fifteen minutes.

Wild Rice Flan

Thinking that it was a grain, not the grass seed that it really is, French explorers first called wild rice "crazy oats." It's harvested from our northern lakes, but it adds a nutty flavor and intriguing texture to a Southwestern dish like flan. Because the rice keeps soaking up liquid, this ends up as a solid flan, with a lovely caramel cap sitting on top of it.

Caramel
¹/₄ cup water
1 cup sugar

Custard
3¹/₂ cups milk
³/₄ cup sugar

¹/₂ cup long-grain white rice
¹/₂ vanilla bean, split
¹/₄ cup wild rice
1 large egg
3 large egg yolks
2 teaspoons vanilla extract

1. THE CARAMEL: Put the water and sugar together in a small heavy-bottomed saucepan. Stir once and cook over high heat until the syrup turns a light amber color. Immediately divide the caramel syrup among 8 completely dry 6-ounce custard cups. Taking care not to touch the hot caramel, swirl the syrup to coat the bottoms and halfway up the sides of the cups.

2. THE CUSTARD: Combine 2¹/₂ cups of the milk, the sugar, and white rice in a medium heavy-bottomed saucepan. Scrape the seeds from the vanilla bean into the milk, add the bean, and bring to a boil over medium heat. Stir, cover, and cook over low heat, stirring from time to time to make sure the bottom isn't

burning, for 45 minutes, or until the mixture looks like soupy porridge. Remove from the heat.

3. Meanwhile, bring a medium saucepan of water to a boil. Add the wild rice, reduce the heat, and boil gently until tender, about 40 minutes. Drain, and set aside.

4. Set a rack in the middle of the oven and preheat to 300°F.

5. Put the remaining 1 cup milk, the egg, yolks, and vanilla in a medium bowl and whisk just to blend. Remove the vanilla bean from the rice, and gradually whisk the rice mixture into the eggs. Stir in the wild rice. Divide the custard among the caramel-coated cups.

6. Put the cups in a roasting pan and add enough hot water to come halfway up the sides of the cups. Tightly cover the pan with foil and bake for 35 to 45 minutes: The custards are ready when they still jiggle slightly when gently shaken but their surface is smooth and set. Let cool to room temperature in the water bath, then remove and refrigerate for at least 8 hours, or overnight.

7. To unmold, run a thin knife between the custard and the inside of each cup. Place a serving plate upside down over the cup and flip the whole thing over with a sharp shake. If the flan doesn't come right out, shake it a few more times. Serve immediately.

Makes 8 individual flans
Store for up to 3 days in the refrigerator.

Note: You can also make one large flan in a shallow five-cup baking dish. Increase the baking time by fifteen minutes.

Sylvester Graham's Mango-Raspberry Cup Custard

During the late nineteenth century, a pre-tofu health food movement spread across the country. Kellogg invented cornflakes in Battle Creek, Michigan, and, on the corner of Pearl and King streets in Northampton, Massachusetts, a fellow by the name of Sylvester Graham invented a flour and a cracker called . . .

Typical of many Southwestern desserts, this dish is a combination of Yankee and South of the Border cooking: A graham cracker crumb crust lines ramekins of mango- and raspberry-studded custard.

Crust

1/2 cup graham cracker crumbs

1 tablespoon sugar

2 tablespoons unsalted butter, melted

Custard

1 1/2 cups milk

1 1/2 cups heavy cream

3/4 cup sugar

1 teaspoon vanilla extract

1 tablespoon framboise (see Note)

8 large egg yolks

1 mango, peeled, pitted, and cut into 1/2-inch chunks

1/2 pint raspberries

1. Set a rack in the middle of the oven and preheat to 300°F. Using 1 tablespoon of the butter, lightly grease the bottoms of eight 6-ounce cups.

2. THE CRUST: Combine the graham cracker crumbs and sugar in a small bowl. Stir

in the remaining 2 tablespoons butter and mix well. Divide the mixture among eight 6-ounce custard cups, pressing it into the bottom of each cup to form a thin crust that comes about one quarter of the way up the sides.

3. THE CUSTARD: In a medium heavy-bottomed saucepan combine the milk, cream, and 1 tablespoon of the sugar. Bring to a scald.

4. Meanwhile, put the remaining sugar ($^1/_2$ cup plus 3 tablespoons), the vanilla, framboise, and egg yolks in a large bowl and whisk just to blend.

5. While gently whisking the yolks, drizzle the hot cream mixture into them so that they are gradually warmed up. Strain the custard into a pitcher.

6. Taking care not to disturb the crust (try drizzling it down a spoon into the cups), pour the custard into the cups. Skim off any bubbles that have formed on the surface. Divide the mango chunks and raspberries among the cups, dunking them so that they are coated with the custard.

7. Put the cups in a roasting pan and add enough hot water to come halfway up the sides of the cups. Tightly cover the pan with foil and bake for 35 to 45 minutes: The custards are ready when they still jiggle slightly when gently shaken but their surface is smooth and set. Let cool to room temperature in the water bath, then remove and refrigerate for at least 4 hours, or overnight, before serving.

Serves 8
**Store for up to 24 hours in the refrigerator,
before brûléing them.**

Note: Framboise, raspberry eau-de-vie, is available at better liquor stores. If you can't find it, substitute an additional teaspoon of vanilla extract.

Pumpkin Crème Brûlée

Pumpkins were grown throughout Arizona and New Mexico long before the arrival of the Spanish. Apache Indians sliced them into big rings and dried them for the winter. With its creamy interior and crunchy crust, crème brûlée is the most luxurious of all custards. Several versions of it are served in Spain in the guise of the popular dessert *crema catalana*. Act fast and plop the pumpkin seeds on while the caramel is still sticky: it quickly sets to a glassy hardness.

3 cups heavy cream
1 cup sugar
$^3/_4$ cup pumpkin puree
   (canned is fine)
1 teaspoon vanilla extract
1 teaspoon cinnamon

$^1/_2$ teaspoon ground cloves
$^1/_4$ teaspoon freshly grated
   nutmeg
8 large egg yolks
$^1/_4$ cup shelled pumpkin seeds

1. Set one rack in the upper third of the oven and another in the lower third, and preheat to 300°F.
2. In a medium heavy-bottomed saucepan, combine the cream and 1 tablespoon of the sugar, and bring to a scald.
3. Meanwhile, put $^1/_2$ cup plus 3 tablespoons sugar, the pumpkin, vanilla, cinnamon, cloves, nutmeg, and egg yolks in a large bowl and whisk just to blend.
4. While gently whisking the yolks, drizzle the hot cream mixture into them so that they are gradually warmed up. Strain the custard into a pitcher, then pour it into eight 6-ounce custard cups. Skim off any bubbles that have formed on the surface.

5. Put the cups in a roasting pan and add enough hot water to come halfway up the sides of the cups. Tightly cover the pan with foil, place on the upper oven rack, and bake for 35 to 45 minutes: The custards are ready when they still jiggle slightly when gently shaken but their surface is smooth and set. Let cool to room temperature in the water bath. Then remove and refrigerate for at least 4 hours, or overnight.

6. Meanwhile, don't waste that hot oven: While the custards are baking, spread the pumpkin seeds on a cookie sheet and toast on the bottom oven rack for 10 minutes, or until you can hear them popping for 1 minute. Remove and let cool.

7. OK, hombre, . . . reach for your propane torch! Just before serving, sprinkle a thin layer of the remaining $1/4$ cup sugar on top of each custard. Slowly run the tip of the torch flame over to melt. Sprinkle on the remaining sugar and melt it to create a glassy caramel top. Quickly sprinkle 1 tablespoon of the pumpkin seeds over each one. Let the caramel set for 1 minute.

Serves 8
Store for up to 24 hours in the refrigerator
before brûléing them.

Kahlúa Chocolate Pudding

Real chocolate pudding takes a bit of work but is well worth the effort. To ensure a nice smooth consistency, take care not to overcook, and make sure that your melted chocolate is still warm when you fold it in.

4 ounces semisweet chocolate,
  coarsely chopped
2 tablespoons unsalted butter
2 tablespoons cornstarch
¹/₄ cup unsweetened cocoa
  powder

³/₄ cup sugar
3¹/₂ cups milk
2 large eggs
3 large egg yolks
¹/₄ cup Kahlúa

1. Melt the chocolate and butter in the top of a double boiler over barely simmering water or in a small bowl set over a saucepan of just-simmering water. Remove from the heat.

2. In a medium bowl, whisk the cornstarch, cocoa, and ¹/₄ cup of the sugar into ¹/₂ cup of the milk.

3. In a medium heavy-bottomed saucepan, combine the remaining 3 cups milk and ¹/₂ cup sugar and bring just to a scald over medium heat. Whisk the hot liquid into the cornstarch mixture, then return the mixture to the saucepan and cook, whisking constantly and scraping the bottom of the pan, until tiny bubbles boil up for 10 seconds. Remove from the heat.

4. Put the eggs and egg yolks into the medium bowl. Whisking gently but constantly, slowly drizzle 1 cup of the hot liquid into them. Return everything to the

saucepan and cook, whisking constantly and scraping the bottom of the pan, until tiny bubbles boil up for 3 seconds. Remove from the heat and stir in the Kahlúa.

5. Strain the pudding through a fine sieve into a bowl. Thoroughly stir in the melted chocolate mixture.

6. Divide the pudding among 8 serving bowls. Place a piece of wax paper directly on the surface of each one to prevent a skin from forming. Let cool for 2 to 3 hours, then refrigerate until chilled.

Serves 8

Store for up to 4 days in the refrigerator.

Lemon-Lime Natilla with Roasted Pine Nuts

Vanilla and orange mellow out the tartness of lemons and limes to make a creamy yet tangy pudding. Pine nuts on top add a toasty contrast.

$^1/_4$ cup cornstarch

$1^1/_4$ cups light cream

2 large eggs

6 large egg yolks

$1^1/_4$ cups sugar

Grated zest of 3 limes

Grated zest of 3 lemons

$^3/_4$ cup fresh lime juice
(5 to 6 limes)

$^1/_2$ cup fresh lemon juice
(3 lemons)

$1^1/_4$ cups fresh orange juice

1 teaspoon vanilla extract

$^1/_2$ cup toasted pine nuts
(see page xxi)

1. Whisk the cornstarch and cream together in a medium bowl. Whisk in the eggs and yolks.

2. In a medium saucepan, combine the sugar, zests, fruit juices, and vanilla and bring to a boil over medium heat. Whisking constantly, slowly drizzle half of the hot liquid into the cream mixture, then return everything to the saucepan and cook, whisking constantly and scraping the bottom of the pan, until tiny bubbles boil up for 10 seconds. Strain the pudding through a fine sieve into a bowl.

3. Divide the pudding among 6 serving bowls. Let cool for 1 hour, then refrigerate until set and chilled.

4. Just before serving, sprinkle on the toasted pine nuts.

Serves 6

Store for up to 3 days in the refrigerator.

Chocolate Ancho Spoonbread

Spoonbread is a lot like a cornmeal soufflé, but it's baked in a casserole. Cooking white cornmeal into a mush, or polenta, turns it as smooth as pastry cream. This down-home soufflé can be reheated one day in advance, but it is at its chocolaty best, hot and puffy, straight from the oven. Serve it with Vanilla Custard Sauce (page 194) or Whipped Cream (page 199).

Melted butter or nonstick
    vegetable spray for greasing
    the pan
8 ounces bittersweet chocolate,
    coarsely chopped
2 tablespoons unsalted butter
2¹/4 cups milk
¹/2 cup white cornmeal

6 large eggs
³/4 cup sugar
2 teaspoons pure ancho chile
    powder
³/4 teaspoon baking powder
¹/8 teaspoon cayenne
¹/4 teaspoon salt

1. Set a rack in the middle of the oven and preheat to 375°F. Lightly grease a shallow 2-quart baking dish.
2. Melt the chocolate and butter in a large bowl set over a saucepan of barely simmering water. Remove from the heat and set aside in a warm place.
3. In a medium saucepan, bring the milk to a scald. Stirring constantly with a wooden spoon, sprinkle in the cornmeal. Reduce the heat to low and cook, stirring occasionally, for 10 minutes until no longer grainy. Remove from the heat.
4. Combine the eggs and sugar in a large bowl, set it over the pan of simmering

water, and increase the heat slightly. Whisk until the eggs are sticky and as warm as bathwater. Don't let them get too hot, or they will scramble. Remove the eggs from the heat and whisk (you can switch to an electric mixer) until they are tripled in volume and form soft peaks.

5. Fold the cooked cornmeal into the chocolate. Fold in one third of the beaten eggs. Sprinkle the ancho chile powder, baking powder, cayenne, and salt over the chocolate mixture, then fold in the remainder of the eggs. Scrape into the baking dish.

6. Bake for 30 minutes, or until puffy and set. Serve hot.

Serves 8
The batter may be prepared through step 5 up to 24 hours in advance, and then refrigerated until ready to bake.

Torejas

Mexican vaqueros were the first cowboys, modeling their riding gear and outfits on the ones used by the conquistadors. Similar Western saddles and wide-brimmed hats eventually became standard equipment for cowpunchers on this side of the border. As we cross the Rio Grande, food styles too can become variations on the same theme. We think of French toast for breakfast, but in Spain, Latin America, and the Southwest it can be a sweet dessert.

Serve this Torejas French toast with ice cream and Cajeta (page 198), a fruit sauce (pages 190–192), or a salsa (pages 178–185).

Melted butter or nonstick vegetable spray for greasing the pan
6 slices brioche or challah bread, crusts trimmed and cut ³/₄ inch thick
¹/₂ cup milk
¹/₂ cup heavy cream
2 tablespoons sugar

2 large eggs
2 large egg yolks
1 teaspoon vanilla extract
1 tablespoon Myers's or other dark rum
1 teaspoon cinnamon
¹/₂ teaspoon freshly grated nutmeg

1. One day in advance, lay the bread out on a cookie sheet to dry and become stale so it will be nice and absorbent.

2. Set a rack in the middle of the oven and preheat to 375°F. Lightly grease a cookie sheet.

3. In a medium bowl, whisk all of the remaining ingredients to blend. Dip 2 to 3 slices of bread in and soak thoroughly, about 5 minutes, then turn and soak the other side. Shake off the excess liquid and lay the slices on the cookie sheet.

4. Bake for 12 minutes, or until just golden and crusty on the top, but still moist and custardy inside. Serve warm.

Serves 6

Lemon Meringue Bread Pudding

Zippy citrus curd with a light meringue topping is the perfect follow-up to a spicy Southwestern main course. Placing it on top of a moist slice of *torejas* turns it into a home-style bread pudding.

Lemon Curd

1 tablespoon cornstarch

$^{1}/_{2}$ cup heavy cream

2 large eggs

4 large egg yolks

Grated zest of 1 lemon

$^{3}/_{4}$ cup fresh lemon juice

$^{1}/_{2}$ cup fresh orange juice

$^{3}/_{4}$ cup sugar

4 tablespoons unsalted butter

$^{1}/_{2}$ teaspoon vanilla extract

Meringue

5 large egg whites

$^{1}/_{2}$ cup sugar

$^{1}/_{4}$ teaspoon salt

Pinch of cream of tartar

1 recipe Torejas (page 98),
   made without cinnamon,
   nutmeg, and rum
   (see Step 4)

1. THE CURD: Whisk the cornstarch and cream together in a medium bowl. Whisk in the eggs and yolks.

2. In a medium nonreactive saucepan, combine the zest, fruit juices, sugar, vanilla, and butter, and bring to a boil over medium heat. Whisking constantly, slowly drizzle half of the hot liquid into the cream mixture. Return everything to

the saucepan and cook, whisking constantly and scraping the bottom of the pan, until tiny bubbles boil up for 10 seconds. Strain the curd through a fine sieve into a bowl, cover with waxed paper, and set aside. (The curd can be prepared up to 1 day in advance and refrigerated.)

3. THE MERINGUE: Place the egg whites, sugar, salt, and cream of tartar in a large stainless steel bowl and set it over a saucepan of simmering water. Whisk constantly until the mixture is lukewarm. Remove from the heat and whisk (you can switch to an electric mixer) until the egg whites form high peaks, like shaving cream.

4. Preheat the oven to 375°F. Prepare and bake the Torejas.

5. Spread the lemon curd over the still-warm Torejas. With the back of a spoon, pile the meringue on top of the curd, pulling up wisps of meringue with the spoon as you go. Set the pudding under a preheated broiler for a few seconds, or pass the flame of a propane torch over the meringue, until lightly browned in spots.

Serves 6
Store for up to 24 hours in the refrigerator.

Chocolate Custard Corn Pone

Derived from the Algonquin Indian word *apan*, corn pone is an old name used to describe the corn bread made by early colonists. For this dessert, I make a chocolate corn bread, soak it in a chocolate custard mixture, and then bake it into a rich, moist chocolate bread pudding. It's thick and voluptuous with the true grit of a homey New England Indian pudding and the kick of Southwestern ancho chile. Serve with Whipped Cream (page 199).

Melted butter or nonstick
  vegetable spray for greasing
  the pan

Chocolate Corn Bread

3 ounces semisweet chocolate,
  coarsely chopped
1 tablespoon unsalted butter
$1/2$ cup all-purpose flour
$1/2$ cup white cornmeal
$1/4$ cup sugar
1 tablespoon pure ancho chile
  powder

1 teaspoon baking powder
$1/4$ teaspoon salt
2 large eggs
$1/2$ cup buttermilk

Custard

4 ounces semisweet chocolate,
  coarsely chopped
2 cups milk
1 cup heavy cream
$1/2$ cup sugar
6 large egg yolks

1. THE CORN BREAD: Set a rack in the middle of the oven and preheat to 375°F. Lightly grease a 9-inch round cake pan. Line it with a disk of parchment paper or buttered waxed paper.

2. Melt the chocolate and butter in the top of a double boiler over barely simmering water or in a small bowl set over a saucepan of just-simmering water. Remove from the heat.

3. Put the flour, cornmeal, sugar, chile powder, baking powder, and salt in a large bowl and stir together with a whisk. Stir in the eggs and buttermilk, then stir in the chocolate mixture.

4. Spread the batter evenly in the prepared pan. Bake for 20 minutes, or until set and a tester comes out clean. Cool in the pan on a wire rack.

5. Break the corn bread into 1-inch chunks. Spread in a shallow 2-quart baking dish.

6. THE CUSTARD: Preheat the oven to 300°F. Melt the chocolate in the top of a double boiler over barely simmering water or in a small bowl set over a saucepan of just-simmering water. Remove from the heat.

7. In a medium heavy-bottomed saucepan, combine the milk, cream, and 1 tablespoon of the sugar and bring to a scald.

8. Meanwhile, put the remaining sugar ($^1/_4$ cup plus 3 tablespoons) and the egg yolks in a large bowl and whisk just to blend. While gently whisking the yolks, drizzle the hot cream mixture into them so that they are gradually warmed up. Whisk in the melted chocolate.

9. Using a fine sieve, strain the custard over the corn bread chunks. Wiggle the chunks around so they are well soaked. Place the baking dish in a roasting pan and add enough hot water to come halfway up the sides of the dish. Bake for 40 minutes, or until the custard is set.

Serves 6 to 8
Store for up to 3 days in the refrigerator;
reheat before serving.

TORTILLA DESSERTS

The Golden Fried West

Crispy Fried Tortillas

The lure of the West: elbow room, adventure, gold, and crunchy fried tortillas. You can buy them in the store, but they are fresher and better if you fry your own. If you have to cut your tortillas down to size for a particular recipe, just put them on a cutting board and, using a plate as a template, slice around it with the tip of a sharp paring knife.

1. Two hours in advance, unwrap the tortillas and spread them out so they can dry. This will prevent them from splattering.

2. In a skillet or electric fryer, heat 1 inch of oil to 375°F. (If you don't have a thermometer, when the oil is hot enough, a tiny drop of water will "explode.")

3. Drop a tortilla into the hot oil and hold it submerged with a pair of tongs for 20 seconds. Then continue to fry for 1 to 2 minutes, until it turns golden brown and floats to the top of the oil, surrounded by a thin ring of tiny bubbles. Flip the tortilla over and fry for 30 seconds to tan the other side. Drain on paper towels. Repeat with the remaining tortillas.

Chocolate Piki Bread

Wafer-thin and crisp, piki is the traditional flatbread of the Hopi and an ancestor of the tortilla. Authentic piki is baked on a hot stone, greased with charred watermelon seeds and lamb's brains (yech)! Our variation, baked in the oven, is flavored with chocolate and orange. Break it into irregular strips and serve it on top of ice cream for a dramatic presentation.

Melted butter or nonstick
  vegetable spray for greasing
  the pan
1 cup all-purpose flour
1 cup unsweetened cocoa
  powder
$^1/_2$ cup sugar

$^1/_4$ cup fine yellow cornmeal
$1^1/_4$ cups strong coffee, cooled
  to room temperature
$^1/_2$ cup orange liqueur
  (Grand Marnier, Cointreau,
  or Triple Sec)

1. Set a rack in the middle of the oven and preheat to 350°F. Lightly grease a 12- by 18-inch cookie sheet to anchor the paper, and line it with parchment paper or waxed paper. Grease the paper.
2. Put the flour, cocoa, sugar, and cornmeal in a large bowl and stir together with a whisk. Gradually whisk in the coffee and orange liqueur until smooth.
3. With an offset metal spatula, spread half of the batter onto the cookie sheet in an even $^1/_{16}$-inch-thick layer. Bake for 15 minutes, or until crisp. Set on a rack

to cool, then repeat with the remaining batter. (Yes, you do have to grease a new piece of paper.) To serve, break into pieces. Piki keeps 1 week in dry weather, but may be recrisped in a 300° oven for 4 minutes.

Makes two 12-inch by 18-inch sheets
Keeps up to 1 week in an airtight container.

Banana-Coconut Custard Tostada

Crunchy cinnamon tostadas form the crusts of these individual coconut custard "tarts." They are also decked out with a top layer of ripe bananas.

2 tablespoons cornstarch
1 1/2 cups milk
4 large egg yolks
1/2 cup sugar
1 teaspoon vanilla extract
1 cup shredded coconut

Six 6-inch Crispy Fried
    Tortillas (see page 105)
1 teaspoon cinnamon
4 large ripe bananas, sliced
    1/4 inch thick

1. In a medium bowl, thoroughly whisk the cornstarch into 1/2 cup of the milk. Let rest for 1 minute, then whisk again. Whisk in the egg yolks.

2. In a medium saucepan, combine the remaining 1 cup milk, 1/2 cup of the sugar, and the vanilla, and bring to a scald over medium heat. Whisking constantly, slowly drizzle the hot liquid into the egg mixture.

3. Return the mixture to the saucepan and cook over medium heat, whisking constantly and scraping the bottom of the pan, until tiny bubbles boil up for 10 seconds. Strain through a fine strainer into a bowl and let cool to room temperature. Cover and refrigerate until chilled and ready to use. (The custard can be refrigerated for up to 2 days.)

4. Set a rack in the middle of the oven and preheat to 350°F.

5. Spread the coconut on a cookie sheet and toast in the oven for 6 minutes, or until lightly tanned. Let cool. (Leave the oven on.)

6. Place the tortillas on an ungreased cookie sheet. Mix the cinnamon and the remaining 2 tablespoons sugar together and sprinkle it over them. Bake for 4 minutes, or until the sugar just melts.

7. Spread a $^1/_4$-inch-thick layer of custard on the tortillas. Arrange sliced bananas in a circle around the edge of the tortillas. Mound the coconut in the center, and serve.

Makes 6 tostadas

Chocolate-Banana Tostada

6 six-inch Crispy Fried
 Tortillas (see page 105)
1 cup shredded coconut
$^1/_2$ recipe Kahlúa Chocolate
 Pudding (page 92)

4 large underripe bananas,
 sliced $^1/_4$ inch thick

Follow the instructions for Banana-Coconut Custard Tostada, beginning with step 4, and substitute the pudding for the vanilla custard.

Rum Raisin Natilla

In England it is called blancmange, across most of America it is vanilla pudding, but the Southwestern version is natilla.

3 tablespoons cornstarch

2 cups milk

3/4 cup sugar

1/4 cup Myers's or other
   dark rum

1 tablespoon vanilla extract

6 large egg yolks

1 cup raisins

1. In a medium bowl, thoroughly whisk the cornstarch into 1/2 cup of the milk. Let rest for 1 minute, then whisk again. Whisk in the egg yolks.

2. In a medium saucepan, combine the remaining 1 1/2 cups milk, the sugar, rum, and vanilla and bring to a scald over medium heat. Whisking constantly, slowly drizzle the hot liquid into the egg mixture.

3. Return the mixture to the saucepan and cook over medium heat, whisking constantly and scraping the bottom of the pan, until tiny bubbles boil up for 10 seconds. Strain through a fine strainer into a bowl. Fold in the raisins.

4. Divide the pudding among 6 serving bowls. Let cool to room temperature, then cover and refrigerate until chilled.

Serves 6

Store for up to 3 days in the refrigerator.

Buñuelos Banana Split

A different kind of sundae—this has crunchy cinnamon tortillas stuck in the top. It's like having a banana split topped with sheets of chocolate-drenched ice cream cone.

Six 6-inch Crispy Fried
    Tortillas (see page 105)
1 teaspoon cinnamon
2 tablespoons sugar

1 quart ice cream, any flavor
3 ripe bananas, sliced
Tia Maria Chocolate Sauce
    (page 188)

1. Set a rack in the middle of the oven and preheat to 350°F.

2. Place the tortillas on an ungreased cookie sheet. Mix the cinnamon and sugar together and sprinkle it over them. Bake for 4 minutes, or until the sugar just melts. With a heavy knife, split the tortillas in half.

3. Place 2 scoops of ice cream on each of 6 dessert plates. Cut a small notch in the top of each scoop and press a tortilla half into it. Garnish with the banana slices, and drizzle on the chocolate sauce.

Makes 6 banana splits

Espresso-Mascarpone Quesadillas with Mixed Fruit

Calling mascarpone Italian cream cheese (which it actually is) is sort of like calling Baryshnikov a guy who dances on his toes. It is sweet and delicate, but luscious. Flavoring it with espresso, sandwiching it between two crunchy cinnamon tortillas, and topping it with fresh fruit makes a perfect summer dessert.

3 tablespoons instant espresso powder

One 500-gram container mascarpone (approximately 2 cups)

1/2 cup confectioners' sugar

Twelve 4-inch Crispy Fried Tortillas (see page 105)

1 teaspoon cinnamon

2 tablespoons sugar

2 cups mixed berries or other fruit cut into bite-sized bits

1. In a medium bowl, dissolve the espresso powder in 2 teaspoons of hot water. Mix the mascarpone and confectioners' sugar and fold in the dissolved espresso powder with a rubber spatula. Cover and chill for at least 1 hour, or overnight.
2. Set a rack in the middle of the oven and preheat to 350°F.
3. Place the tortillas on an ungreased cookie sheet. Mix the cinnamon and sugar together and sprinkle it over them. Bake for 4 minutes, or until the sugar just melts.

4. Just before serving, spread the flavored mascarpone on 6 of the tortillas. Arrange the berries or fruit on the mascarpone, and then place the remaining tortillas on top, sugared side up.

Makes 6 quesadillas

Note: Try one of the fruit salsas as a substitute for the berries or fruit in this recipe. I especially like the Strawberry-Almond (page 178). Raspberry-Cherimoya Chip (page 179), Apricot-Hazelnut (page 182), or Chocolate Raspberry (page 184) with the mascarpone.

Warm Chocolate Pudding Enchiladas

Crêpes are delicate but turn dry when baked. Blintz wrappers are moist but, unless fried, can be a bit rubbery. Borrowing the best from both gives us a thin, pliable pancake to wrap around our chocolate pudding. Bake this enchilada just long enough to warm the pudding up, then watch it ooze out as you cut into it. Serve with Whipped Cream (page 199) and Strawberry-Almond Salsa (page 178).

Enchiladas
3/4 cup all-purpose flour
1/4 cup plus 2 tablespoons
  unsweetened cocoa powder
2 tablespoons sugar

1 1/4 cups milk
2 large eggs

1/2 recipe Kahlúa Chocolate
  Pudding (page 92)

1. THE ENCHILADAS: Put all of the ingredients except the pudding in a food processor fitted with the metal blade or a blender and process for 1 minute. Scrape down the sides of the container and process for 10 seconds. Transfer the batter to a bowl and let rest in the refrigerator for 30 minutes.

2. Heat a nonstick crêpe pan or sauté pan over medium-high heat for 1 minute. Add 1/4 cup of the batter to the pan, tilting it so the batter coats the bottom in a thin film. Pour any excess batter back into the bowl, and cook the pancake for about 2 minutes, until the top looks set but not dry and you can lift up the pancake with a rubber spatula and your fingers (get an edge started with the spatula and your fingers can do the rest—it's not that hot).

3. Place the pancake cooked side up on a sheet of waxed paper, and repeat with the remaining batter, for a total of 6 pancakes. Stack the pancakes between sheets of waxed paper.

4. Preheat the oven to 400°F. Lightly butter a cookie sheet.

5. Place a pancake, cooked side up, on a work surface. Plop $1/4$ cup of the pudding about one third of the way up from the bottom. Spread it into a rectangle across the pancake, leaving 1-inch borders. Fold the bottom of the pancake up over the pudding, then fold over the sides. Roll the enchilada up and place seam side down on the prepared cookie sheet. Repeat with the other remaining pancakes and pudding. (The enchiladas can be prepared up to 1 day in advance to this point.) Cover and refrigerate.

6. Bake the enchiladas for 5 to 7 minutes, just until warmed through. Serve immediately.

Makes 6 enchiladas
Enchiladas can be prepared up to 6 hours in advance.

COOKIES

High Noon at the Cookie Jar

The pottery produced in the Southwest is among the most beautiful in the world, but sometimes it's the cookie jar that gets all the attention. Both Mexicans and Americans are expert cookie makers: Small wonder that so many little banditos meet for the big showdown over a big stack of freshly baked cookies.

1. A small ice cream scoop works great for forming drop cookies.

2. Don't plop your cookies out in a wild stampede. A planned, staggered pattern will conserve room and help prevent cookies from "marrying" each other as they spread.

3. Roll sticky cookie doughs between sheets of waxed paper.

4. The best way to chill shaped cookies is on a sheet of parchment paper. Then, to bake, transfer the whole sheet to a room-temperature cookie sheet. Don't plop cold dough onto a hot sheet pan: the butter will melt out before the cookies solidify.

5. To maintain neat shapes, lift cut cookies onto their pan with a metal spatula.

6. Don't fiddle around with cookies until they are cooled down and set; you could end up with scrunched-up lumps of dough.

7. Of course you can change the size of your cookies: bigger, smaller, different shapes. Go right ahead.

Blue Corn Biscotti

Two different cornmeals give these biscotti a wonderful crunchy texture. They also help to keep that crunch after a dunking in espresso or dessert wine.

2¹/₂ cups all-purpose flour

1¹/₄ cups sugar

2 tablespoons yellow cornmeal

¹/₄ cup plus 2 tablespoons blue
  cornmeal

1¹/₂ teaspoons baking powder

¹/₂ teaspoon salt

³/₄ cup (1¹/₂ ounces) pecan
  pieces

8 tablespoons (1 stick)
  unsalted butter, at room
  temperature

2 large eggs

2 tablespoons anisette or
  sambuca

1. Set a rack in the middle of the oven and preheat to 375°F.

2. Put the flour, sugar, yellow and blue cornmeal, baking powder, salt, and pecans in the bowl of an electric mixer and stir together with a fork. With the mixer at its slowest speed, beat in the butter bit by bit until blended. Add the eggs and liqueur, and beat until the dough is thoroughly blended and masses together.

3. Transfer the dough out to a floured work surface, and shape it into a log 3 inches wide, 12 inches long, and 1 inch high. Place it on a parchment paper–lined or nonstick baking sheet pan.

4. Bake for 30 minutes, or until lightly browned. Let cool on the baking sheet for at least 2 hours, or overnight.

5. Preheat the oven to 350°F.

6. Transfer the dough log to a cutting board. With a serrated knife, slice the log into ¹/₂-inch slices, and lay them on the baking sheet. Bake for 10 to 12 minutes, until lightly browned around the edges. After 6 minutes turn the pan from front to back if they are not browning evenly. Cool on the cookie sheet on a wire rack.

Makes about 2 dozen cookies
Store for up to 2 weeks in a cookie jar.

Note: Rolling the dough into a log may cause bubbles and air spaces in the dough, so it's better to "press" it into shape.

Dried Cherry and Hazelnut Toll House Cookies

There are three types of cookie eaters: (1) hard cookie aficionados; (2) lovers of the soft; and (3) those who can't wait and eat the batter raw. Most people belong to all three groups, so these cookies are soft in the center and crunchy on the edges. (Whatever goes on between you and that glob of raw dough is your own business.)

³/4 cup (3 ounces) dried cherries

¹/4 cup water

1¹/4 cups all-purpose flour

³/4 teaspoon baking powder

¹/4 teaspoon baking soda

¹/4 teaspoon salt

8 tablespoons (1 stick) unsalted butter, at room temperature

³/4 cup lightly packed dark brown sugar

¹/4 cup granulated sugar

1 large egg

2 teaspoons vanilla extract

2 tablespoons Frangelico (see Notes)

³/4 cup (4 ounces) skinned and roasted hazelnuts (see Notes)

³/4 cup semisweet chocolate chips

1. Combine the cherries and water in a small saucepan and bring to a simmer. Remove from the heat, and let the cherries cool in the liquid. Drain well.
2. Set a rack in the middle of the oven and preheat to 375°F.
3. Put the flour, baking powder, baking soda, and salt in a medium bowl and stir together with a whisk.

4. Combine the butter and sugar in the bowl of an electric mixer and beat at medium speed for 30 seconds, or until smooth. Add the egg and beat until just fluffy, about 1 minute. Turn the mixer down to its lowest setting and add the flour mixture in 3 stages, beating just enough to combine. Add the vanilla and Frangelico. Then mix in the hazelnuts, chocolate chips, and cherries.

5. Drop the dough by walnut-sized balls at least 3 inches apart onto a parchment paper–lined or nonstick cookie sheet. (These things spread, and I mean it, so allow ample space.) With moistened fingers, slightly flatten the cookies.

6. Bake for 12 minutes, turning the pan once for even baking, until the cookies are lightly browned, but still soft in the center.

Makes about 2 dozen 3-inch cookies
Store for up to 1 week in a cookie jar or freeze,
well wrapped, for up to 1 month.

Notes: Frangelico is a hazelnut liqueur available in most liquor stores. In a pinch, you can substitute dark rum.

Hazelnuts are sold three ways: Skinned and roasted are ready to go. Blanched (skinless) should be roasted in a 350°F oven for 6 minutes, or until tanned. Raw should be roasted at 350°F for 6 minutes and then, when cool enough to handle, rubbed together in a towel to remove the skins.

Pistachio Chocolate Chocolate Chip Cookies

Although they are a new addition to the landscape, pistachio trees love dry, alkaline soil, so they are right at home in the Tularosa Basin of south-central New Mexico. They also taste great with chocolate, so are right at home in these thick, fudgy cookies.

3 ounces semisweet chocolate,
   coarsely chopped
1³/₄ cups all-purpose flour
1 teaspoon baking powder
¹/₄ teaspoon salt
10 tablespoons unsalted butter,
   at room temperature

³/₄ cup sugar
1 large egg
³/₄ cup shelled pistachio nuts
³/₄ cup semisweet chocolate
   chips

1. Set a rack in the middle of the oven and preheat to 375°F.
2. Melt the chopped chocolate in the top of a double boiler over barely simmering water or in a small bowl set over a saucepan of just-simmering water. Remove from the heat.
3. Put the flour, baking powder, and salt in a medium bowl and stir together with a whisk.
4. Combine the butter and sugar in the bowl of an electric mixer. Beat at medium speed for 30 seconds, or until smooth. Add the egg and beat until not quite

fluffy, about 1 minute. Turn the mixer down to its lowest setting and beat in the melted chocolate until thoroughly blended. Add the flour mixture in 3 stages, blending just to combine. Mix in the pistachios and chocolate chips.

5. Drop the dough by walnut-sized balls 2½ inches apart onto a parchment paper–lined nonstick cookie sheet. With moistened fingers, flatten the cookies a little bit.

6. Bake, turning the pan once for even baking, for 10 minutes, or until the cookies are just firm around the edges but still soft in the center.

**Makes about 2 dozen 3-inch cookies
Store for up to 1 week in a cookie jar or freeze, well
wrapped, for up to 1 month.**

Polvorones

There is a delicate, luscious, crumbly mound of a cookie called a Mexican wedding cake. These *polvorone*, or "dusty," cookies are made from a similar nutty dough, but rolled out and cut into shapes.

2 cups all-purpose flour
1/2 cup confectioners' sugar
1 cup (2 ounces) finely
   chopped pecans
12 tablespoons (1*1/2* sticks)
   unsalted butter, at room
   temperature

1 large egg
1 tablespoon vanilla extract
1 ounce semisweet chocolate,
   coarsely chopped

1. Set a rack in the middle of the oven and preheat to 375°F.
2. Put the flour, confectioners' sugar, and pecans into the bowl of an electric mixer or a food processor fitted with the metal blade. With the mixer on low speed, beat in the butter bit by bit. Or, pulsing the processor, add the butter bit by bit. Add the egg and vanilla extract, and beat or process until the dough is thoroughly blended and masses together.
3. Roll the dough between 2 sheets of wax paper to a thickness of 1/4 inch. Place on a baking sheet and refrigerate for 30 minutes, or until firm.
4. Peel off the wax paper. Cut out shapes with a cookie cutter or a small knife, placing them on a parchment paper–lined or nonstick cookie sheet. Refrigerate for 10 minutes. Gather together the scraps of dough and reroll.

5. Bake the cookies for 13 minutes, or until very lightly browned around the edges. Cool on the pan on a wire rack.

6. Melt the chocolate in a small bowl set over a saucepan of barely simmering water. With a fork, drizzle chocolate streaks across the cookies.

Makes about 3 dozen $2^1/_2$-inch cookies
Store for up to 4 days, well wrapped, at room temperature.

Note: While the chocolate is still runny, you can drop some toasted pumpkin seeds on top of the cookies. You can also skip the chocolate and just dust the cookies with a little confectioners' sugar and cinnamon.

Peanut Oatmeal Cookies

I am often asked to reveal my secret ingredients, but, more often than not, the secret lies not in the ingredients but in the technique. However, these cookies certainly do have one, and it's maple syrup. Go for the real McCoy rather than the fake stuff: It has a subtle, absolutely luxurious flavor.

1 cup all-purpose flour
1/2 teaspoon baking powder
1/2 teaspoon baking soda
1/4 teaspoon salt
8 tablespoons (1 stick)
  unsalted butter, at room
  temperature
1/2 cup lightly packed light
  brown sugar

1/2 cup granulated sugar
1 large egg
1/4 cup pure maple syrup
1/2 teaspoon vanilla extract
2 cups rolled (old-fashioned)
  oats
1/2 cup roasted unsalted
  peanuts

1. Set a rack in the middle of the oven and preheat to 350°F.
2. Put the flour, baking powder, baking soda, and salt in a medium bowl and stir together with a whisk.
3. Combine the butter and sugar in the bowl of an electric mixer and beat at medium speed for 30 seconds, or until smooth. Add the eggs one at a time, beating until each is incorporated. Continue beating until just fluffy, about 1 minute. Turn the mixer down to its lowest setting and add the flour mixture, blending just to combine. Beat in the maple syrup and vanilla. Then add the oats and peanuts.

4. Drop the batter by walnut-sized balls 2½ inches apart onto a parchment paper–lined or nonstick cookie sheet, staggering the cookies so they don't "marry" each other. With moistened fingers, flatten the cookies a little bit.

5. Bake for 12 minutes, turning the pan once for even baking, until the cookies are lightly browned but still soft in the center. Cool on the pan on a wire rack.

Makes about 30 cookies
Store for up to 1 week in a cookie jar or freeze, well wrapped, for up to 1 month.

Molettes

You can always depend on cornmeal to add texture and character to a cookie. These Mexican cornmeal molettes are a cross between sablés (French butter cookies) and old-fashioned shortenin' bread. The pine nuts, or *piñons*, that we press into the tops were an important staple of Native Americans, especially the Navajo.

12 tablespoons (1¹/₂ sticks) unsalted butter, at room temperature

³/₄ cup lightly packed light brown sugar

1 large egg

¹/₂ teaspoon vanilla extract

2 teaspoons bourbon

¹/₂ cup fine yellow cornmeal

1³/₄ cups all-purpose flour

1 large egg yolk beaten with 2 tablespoons water for egg wash

About ¹/₂ cup pine nuts

1. Set a rack in the middle of the oven and preheat to 375°F.
2. Combine the butter and brown sugar in the bowl of an electric mixer, and beat at medium speed for 30 seconds, or until smooth. Add the egg and beat for 1 minute, or until well blended. Turn the mixer down to its lowest setting and add half of the flour and cornmeal, blending just to combine. Beat in the bourbon and vanilla, then the remaining flour mixture.
3. Roll the dough between 2 sheets of waxed paper to a thickness of ¹/₄ inch. Place on a baking sheet and refrigerate for 30 minutes, or until firm.

4. Cut out shapes with a cookie cutter or a small knife and place them on a parchment paper–lined nonstick cookie sheet. Brush the cookies with the egg wash, and gently press a few pine nuts into each one. Refrigerate the cookies for 10 minutes (this helps to keep their edges sharp).

5. Bake the cookies for about 15 minutes, until very lightly browned around the edges. Cool on the pan on a wire rack.

Makes about 3 dozen cookies
Store for up to 5 days, well wrapped,
at room temperature.

Pecan-Cornmeal Madeleines

Outlaws and other desperado types used to roam the Wild West, wreaking havoc (and/or just plain reeking). After particularly hard days of rustling, bushwacking, and holding up stagecoaches, these hombres and hombrettes would head over to the local saloon, kick the doors open, and proclaim, "It's time to celebrate. Let's have a nice cup of tea."

Madeleines, the classic French accompaniment for tea, are halfway between cakes and cookies. Instead of using traditional seashell madeleine molds, I like to bake these in old corncob-shaped corn bread molds. Try them as après water pistol fight snacks or with ice cream as a full-fledged dessert.

Melted butter or nonstick vegetable spray for greasing the molds
³/₄ cup plus 2 tablespoons all-purpose flour
¹/₄ cup fine yellow cornmeal
¹/₂ teaspoon baking powder
¹/₄ teaspoon salt

¹/₄ cup chopped pecans
8 tablespoons (1 stick) unsalted butter, at room temperature
¹/₂ cup sugar
2 large eggs
1 teaspoon vanilla extract
1 teaspoon bourbon

1. Set a rack in the middle of the oven and preheat to 400°F. Grease a set of corn bread or madeleine molds, making sure that you get every little nook and cranny.

2. Put the flour, cornmeal, baking powder, and salt in a medium bowl and stir together with a whisk. Stir in the pecans.

3. Combine the butter and sugar in the bowl of an electric mixer. Beat at high speed for 30 seconds, or until smooth. Add the eggs one at a time, beating until each is incorporated. Beat until very light and fluffy, about 5 minutes.

4. Turn the mixer down to its lowest setting and beat in half of the flour mixture. Beat in the vanilla and bourbon, then the remaining flour mixture. Spoon the batter into the molds, filling them to the top. Bake for 15 minutes, or until springy to the touch and golden.

5. Let the madeleines cool for 5 minutes, then remove them from the molds by knocking them out with a sharp rap or gently prying them out with a butter knife. Transfer to a rack to cool. Store in an airtight container until serving time.

Makes about 18 cookies
Store up to 2 days in an airtight container
or cookie jar.

Red-Hot Cinnamon Snickerdoodles

When I was a little kid, my Grandpa Sam used to make his own incendiary horse-radish. Sitting at the dining room table, I would watch in utter bewilderment as the grown-ups would dip into the fiery stuff, grimace, gasp, and then tearfully exclaim, "Oh boy, this is good."

The thrill of the sting in spicy foods is like the excitement of a roller coaster ride or a good horror movie: "Scare me more, I love it." Hot and sugary are a natural combination; sweet fire accents other flavors, making them even more pronounced.

2 cups all-purpose flour
2 teaspoons baking powder
1 teaspoon baking soda
2 teaspoons cinnamon
$1/2$ teapoon cayenne
$1/4$ teaspoon salt

8 tablespoons (1 stick)
   unsalted butter, at room
   temperature
$1^1/4$ cups sugar
1 large egg

1. Set a rack in the middle of the oven and preheat to 375°F.
2. Put the flour, baking powder, baking soda, 1 teaspoon of the cinnamon, $1/4$ teaspoon of the cayenne, and the salt in a medium bowl and stir together with a whisk.
3. Combine the butter and 1 cup of the sugar in the bowl of an electric mixer. Beat at medium speed for 30 seconds, or until smooth. Add the egg and beat until

just fluffy, about 1 minute. Turn the mixer down to its lowest setting and add the flour mixture in 3 stages, blending just to combine.

4. Drop the batter, by walnut-sized balls, $2^{1}/_{2}$ inches apart onto a parchment paper–lined, nonstick cookie sheet. With moistened fingers, flatten the cookies a bit.

5. Mix together the remaining $^{1}/_{4}$ cup sugar, $^{1}/_{4}$ teaspoon cinnamon, and $^{1}/_{4}$ teaspoon cayenne, and sprinkle lightly over the cookies. Bake for about 12 minutes, turning the pan once for even baking, until the cookies are evenly browned. Cool on the pan on a rack.

Makes about 2 dozen 3$^{1}/_{2}$-inch cookies
Store for up to 1 week in a cookie jar or freeze, well wrapped, for up to 1 month.

Mexican Brownies

In 1825, Brillat-Savarin, the great-grandpappy of food writing, said that in order for it to be called chocolate, cocoa had to be cooked with sugar and cinnamon. Mexicans, the original chocolate lovers, still like it this way.

These cinnamon and pumpkin seed brownies are the fudgy, gooey, chunky kind. What's the point of having them any other way?

*Melted butter or nonstick
   vegetable spray for greasing
   the pan
$^1/_2$ cup ($2^3/_4$ ounces) shelled
   pumpkin seeds
$^3/_4$ cup raisins
1 cup hot strong coffee
5 ounces bittersweet chocolate,
   coarsely chopped*

*8 tablespoons (1 stick)
   unsalted butter
$^1/_4$ cup all-purpose flour
$^3/_4$ teaspoon baking powder
1 teaspoon cinnamon,
   preferably Mexican canela
$^1/_4$ teaspoon salt
$^1/_2$ cup sugar
2 large eggs*

1. Position a rack in the center of the oven and preheat to 350°F. Grease a 9-inch square cake pan, line the bottom with a square of parchment paper or wax paper, and grease the paper.
2. Spread the pumpkin seeds on a cookie sheet and toast them in the oven until you can hear them pop for 1 whole minute. Let cool.
3. Put the raisins in a small bowl and pour the coffee over them. Set aside to soak.
4. Melt the chocolate and butter in the top of a double boiler over barely simmer-

ing water or in a small bowl set over a saucepan of just-simmering water. Remove from the heat.

5. Sift the flour, baking powder, cinnamon, and salt together onto a sheet of waxed paper. Sift 2 more times to mix and aerate.

6. In a large bowl, lightly whisk the sugar and eggs together, just to blend. Whisk in the chocolate mixture, then whisk in the flour mixture just to blend. Fold in the pumpkin seeds, taking care not to overmix. Drain the raisins, and fold them in.

7. Spread the batter evenly in the prepared pan. Bake for about 18 minutes, until just barely set and a cake tester comes out with moist crumbs. Let cool.

8. Run a thin sharp knife around the edges of the pan, then either flip the slab of brownies over onto a serving platter or serve right out of the pan, cut into squares.

Makes 9 squares
Store for up to 2 days, well wrapped, at room temperature.

Biscochitos

We've all heard of state flowers and state birds, but New Mexico has a state cookie. It's a round anise-flavored shortbread that is made in bakery ovens and *hornos*, the beehive-shaped outdoor ovens found at pueblos all over the Southwest. Genuine biscochito recipes use lard, which accounts for their flakiness. I use butter, but rub it into the dough to achieve the layered texture of the authentic product. Incidentally, New Mexico's state bird is the roadrunner and the state flower is the yucca.

2 cups all-purpose flour
³/4 cup plus 2 tablespoons
  sugar
¹/2 teaspoon baking powder
¹/8 teaspoon salt
1 tablespoon plus ¹/2 teaspoon
  ground anise

12 tablespoons (1¹/2 sticks)
  cold unsalted butter, cut into
  pea-sized bits
1 large egg yolk
1 teaspoon vanilla extract
3 tablespoons ice water

1. Put the flour, ³/4 cup of the sugar, the baking powder, salt, and ¹/2 teaspoon of the anise in a large bowl and whisk to blend. Using a pastry blender or your fingertips, work in the butter until the mixture resembles coarse meal. Add the egg yolk, vanilla, and ice water and mix with your fingers just until the dough comes together into a ball. Working on a lightly floured surface, take egg-sized pieces of the dough and smear them away from you with the heel of your hand into 6-inch streaks. Scrape up all the streaks of dough and pile them on top of one another to form a disk. Wrap in plastic wrap and refrigerate for at least 2 hours, or overnight.

2. On a lightly floured surface, roll the dough to a thickness of $^1/_4$ inch. Refrigerate for 30 minutes, or until firm.

3. Set a rack in the middle of the oven and preheat to 375°F.

4. With a cookie cutter, cut out $2^1/_2$-inch circles, placing them on a parchment paper–lined or nonstick cookie sheet. Reroll the scraps of dough and cut out more cookies. Chill the cookies for 10 minutes.

5. Meanwhile, mix the remaining 1 tablespoon anise and 2 tablespoons sugar together in a small bowl.

6. Sprinkle a thin layer of the sugar mixture over the cookies. Bake for 10 minutes, or until lightly browned around the edges. Cool on the pan on a wire rack.

Makes 2¹/₂ dozen 2¹/₂-inch cookies
Store for up to 5 days, well wrapped,
at room temperature.

Almond Biscochitos

Layers of sliced almonds give these biscochitos an even flakier texture than the plain ones.

1¹/₂ cups all-purpose flour

¹/₂ cup sugar

1 teaspoon baking powder

¹/₈ teaspoon salt

³/₄ cup toasted sliced almonds
   (see page xxi)

12 tablespoons (1¹/₂ sticks)
   cold unsalted butter, cut into
   pea-sized bits

1 large egg yolk

3 tablespoons amaretto

¹/₂ teaspoon almond extract

1. Put the flour, sugar, baking powder, and salt in a large bowl, and whisk to blend. Stir in the almonds. Using a pastry blender or your fingertips, work in the butter until the mixture resembles coarse meal. Add the egg yolk, amaretto, and almond extract, and mix with your fingers just until the dough comes together into a ball. Working on a lightly floured surface, take egg-sized pieces of dough and smear them away from you with the heel of your hand into 6-inch streaks. Scrape up all the dough streaks and pile them on top of one another to form a disk. Wrap in plastic wrap and refrigerate for at least 2 hours, or overnight.

2. On a lightly floured surface, roll the dough to a thickness of ¹/₄ inch. Refrigerate for 30 minutes, or until firm.

3. Set a rack in the middle of the oven and preheat to 375°F.

4. With a cookie cutter, cut out 2½-inch circles, placing them on a parchment paper–lined or nonstick cookie sheet. Reroll the scraps of dough and cut out more cookies. Chill the cookies for 10 minutes.

5. Bake for 10 minutes, or until lightly browned around the edges. Cool on the pan on a wire rack.

Makes 2½ dozen 2½-inch cookies
Store for up to 5 days, well wrapped,
at room temperature.

Lemon Corn Crisps

Crunchy when cool, but pliable while still warm, these crisps can be served flat or shaped into curls, cups, and squiggles. Don't overload yourself with too many cookies at once. Alternate small batches on two cookie sheets. If your cookies harden too quickly, rewarm them briefly in the oven, and they will soften. For the adventurous, try adding the cracked pepper to the batter. Bake these cookies on a nice dry day, as humidity greatly affects how long they will keep.

Melted butter or nonstick
   vegetable spray for greasing
   the pans
3 large egg whites
$^3/_4$ cup sugar
$^1/_4$ cup plus 2 tablespoons all-
   purpose flour
$^1/_4$ cup coarse cornmeal
1 teaspoon vanilla extract

Grated zest of 1 lemon
1 tablespoon fresh lemon juice
$^1/_2$ teaspoon coarse (butcher
   grind) black pepper
   (optional)
4 tablespoons ($^1/_2$ stick)
   unsalted butter, melted and
   cooled to lukewarm

1. Set a rack in the middle of the oven and preheat to 350°F. Lightly grease 2 non-stick cookie sheets.

2. Put the egg whites and sugar in a large mixing bowl and whisk for 1 minute, or until light and foamy. Whisk in the flour, cornmeal, vanilla, lemon zest and juice, and the pepper, if using. Whisk in the melted butter.

3. Drop tablespoons of the batter 6 inches apart onto one of the prepared cookie

sheets, and spread them into 2-inch rounds with the back of the spoon or moistened fingers. Bake, turning the pan once for even baking, for 7 minutes, or until browned around the edges. Set the cookie sheet on a rack to cool for 10 seconds, then gently lift up the cookies one by one with a metal spatula and set on a wire rack to crisp. Bake the remainder of the batter, alternating the two cookie sheets, regreasing the pans for each batch.

Makes 2 dozen cookies
Store for up to 2 days in an airtight container.

Lemon Corn Tiles and Cups

To make tile cookies, or "tuiles," make slightly larger cookies. Using a metal spatula, remove from the pan while warm and pliable, and drape over a rolling pin to crisp.

Makes 18 cookies

Follow the same procedure to make cups, or "tulipes," but double the size of the cookies. Shape by gently pressing the warm cookies inside coffee cups. Use a little more batter to make even larger cups. Be sure to allow room for spreading on the cookie sheet.

Makes 12 cups

Chocolate Hazelnut Crackers

In Italy, chocolate and hazelnuts are a popular combo. These "crackers" are baked as big sheets of chocolate flatbread that can be broken up. They are not overly sweet and make an ideal accompaniment to ice cream or custard.

Melted butter or nonstick
vegetable spray for the pan
1 cup plus 2 tablespoons
all-purpose flour
1 1/2 cups unsweetened cocoa
powder

1/2 cup sugar
3/4 cup finely chopped toasted
hazelnuts (see page xxi)
2 cups coffee, cooled to room
temperature
1/4 cup Frangelico

1. Set a rack in the middle of the oven and preheat to 350°F. Lightly grease a 12- by 18-inch cookie sheet to anchor the paper, and line it with parchment paper or waxed paper. Lightly grease the paper.

2. Put the flour, cocoa, and sugar in a large bowl and stir together with a whisk. Whisk in the nuts. Gradually whisk in the coffee and Frangelico until smooth.

3. With an offset metal spatula, spread half of the batter onto the cookie sheet in an even 1/16-inch-thick layer. Bake for 15 minutes, or until crisp. Set on a rack to cool. Then repeat with the remaining batter (yes, you do have to grease a new piece of paper). To serve, break the sheets into pieces.

Makes two 12- by 18-inch sheets
Store for up to 4 days at room temperature.

Linzer Hearts of the West

Tangy cranberries with a touch of jalapeño add a little fire to spicy linzer tarts. The crusts for these individual tartlets, which we cut out with heart and horse-shaped cookie cutters, can be made in advance. The tartlets are assembled just before serving.

Linzer Crusts

1³/4 cups all-purpose flour
1 cup almonds
³/4 cup confectioners' sugar
1 teaspoon cinnamon
1/4 teaspoon ground cloves
12 tablespoons (1¹/2 sticks)
   unsalted butter, at room
   temperature
1 large egg
1 teaspoon vanilla extract
1 large egg yolk beaten with
   2 tablespoons water for
   egg wash

Cranberry Filling

1/4 cup fresh orange juice
2 tablespoons orange liqueur
   (Grand Marnier, Curaçao, or
   Triple Sec)
1/4 cup plus 2 tablespoons
   sugar
2¹/2 cups fresh or thawed
   frozen cranberries
1/4 teaspoon finely chopped
   jalapeño or serrano chile

Confectioners' sugar for
   dusting

1. THE CRUSTS: Put the flour, almonds, confectioners' sugar, cinnamon, and cloves into the bowl of an electric mixer. With the mixer on low speed, beat in the but-

144

ter bit by bit. Add the egg and vanilla, and beat until the dough is thoroughly blended and masses together. Or, combine the dry ingredients in a food processor fitted with the metal blade. Pulsing the machine, add the butter bit by bit. Add the egg and vanilla, and process until the dough is thoroughly blended and masses together.

2. Divide the dough in half and roll out between 2 sheets of wax paper to a thickness of $1/4$ inch. Place on a baking sheet, and chill for 30 minutes, or until firm.

3. Preheat the oven to 375°F.

4. With $3^1/2$-inch cookie cutters, cut out hearts and horses, placing them on a nonstick or parchment paper–lined cookie sheet. Gather the dough scraps together, reroll, and cut out more cookies, for a total of 8 of each kind. Lightly brush the cookies with the egg wash. Refrigerate for 10 minutes (chilling helps keep the edges sharp).

5. Bake the cookies for 15 minutes, or until lightly browned around the edges. Let cool on the pan on a wire rack.

6. THE FILLING: Combine the orange juice, liqueur, sugar, and cranberries in a nonreactive saucepan. Cook over medium heat, stirring, for 15 minutes, or until the cranberries have burst and softened. Remove from the heat and let cool, then stir in the chile.

7. To assemble, place a heart cookie on each plate and mound about $1/4$ cup of the filling on top. Then stand a horse cookie in the filling, lightly dust the entire dessert with confectioners' sugar, and serve.

Makes 8 tartlets
Store cookies at room temperature, refrigerate filling.

ICE CREAM

Ice Cream Sandwich Roundup

Ice cream and cookies make a darlin' little dessert, but after a hard day on the trail, you can develop a hankerin' for something with a little more bravura. Take the same ingredients and assemble them into a sandwich. All you need are two flat cookies with three little scoops of ice cream slipped in between. Add a sauce or salsa and you've got a showstopper. Here are some combinations to try:

Cookies	Ice Cream
Dried Cherry and Hazelnut Toll House	*Mango, Brown Sugar–Vanilla*
Peanut Oatmeal	*Banana Chocolate Crackle, Canela, Peanut Butter Fudge*
Polvorones	*Mango, Brown Sugar–Vanilla, Piloncillo*
Pistachio Chocolate Chocolate Chip	*Mango*
Biscochitos	*Serrano, Piloncillo*
Almond Biscochitos	*Brown Sugar–Vanilla, Canela*
Molettes	*Fresh Corn, Piloncillo*
Lemon Corn Crisps	*Fresh Corn, Piloncillo, Brown Sugar–Vanilla*
Red-Hot Cinnamon Snickerdoodles	*Sweet Potato, Canela, Serrano*
Chocolate Hazelnut Crackers	*Mango, Sweet Potato, Brown Sugar–Vanilla*

Sundae Outing

Live country and western music extravaganzas in a laundromat? That's what happens every Friday night at Holmes' Coin-O-Mat in Azle, Texas. It's sort of a karaoke version of a *Hee-Haw* rerun with added bleach and fabric softener. Main thing is that the combination works!

Sundaes are all about making up combinations. Ice creams with toppings: sauces, salsas, fresh fruits, nuts. The possibilities go on and on. Here are just a few for starters:

Ice Cream	Sauce or Salsa
Fresh Corn	*Cajeta, Whiskey Butterscotch Sauce*
Piloncillo	*Apricot-Hazelnut Salsa, Blueberry Sauce*
Banana Chocolate Crackle	*Raspberry-Cherimoya Chip Salsa, Tia Maria Chocolate Sauce*
Peanut Butter Fudge	*Chocolate Raspberry Salsa*
Jalapeño	*Melon and Blackberry Salsa, Raspberry Sauce*
Brown Sugar–Vanilla	*Strawberry-Almond Salsa, Cajeta*
Canela	*Apple-Walnut Salsa, Pumpkin Sauce*
Mango	*Strawberry Almond Salsa, Clear Mint Sauce*
Sweet Potato	*Grilled Pineapple with Caramel Sauce*

Ice Cream Pie-

Remember the à la Mode

Instead of just placing a scoop of ice cream alongside a slice of pie, why not fill a crumb crust with ice cream? Use the recipe for Graham Crust on page 48 and fill it with Sweet Potato (page 165), Canela (page 162), or Piloncillo (page 152) ice cream. The Chocolate Pie shell on page 43 is good with Banana Chocolate Crackle (page 154), Mango (page 163), or Peanut Butter Fudge (page 156).

Make sure the crust is cooled down, then completely chill it in the freezer. Fill it with soft ice cream, straight from the ice cream machine, then freeze again. If you are using store-bought ice cream, let it soften slightly in the refrigerator. (If you have to loosen the pie from its plate, pop it in a 350°F oven for just 10 seconds.)

Fresh Corn Ice Cream

With its distinctive sweetness, how come corn isn't as popular an ice cream flavor as vanilla or chocolate? Is there a credibility gap here? Well, I'll pose this question: What substance would you expect to make the most terrific ice cream?

a. unsweetened chocolate (ugh—tastes like aspirin)

b. a black, bitter vanilla bean (which is really a fermented flower)

c. a sweet, delicious ear of freshly picked corn

No contest. Corn has 'em all beat.

3 cups fresh corn kernels
2 cups heavy cream
1/4 cup granulated sugar
2 cups milk

3/4 cup lightly packed light brown sugar
9 large egg yolks
2 tablespoons bourbon

1. Combine the corn, cream, and granulated sugar in a medium saucepan, simmer for 20 minutes. Let cool slightly, then transfer to a food processor and puree. Strain the puree through a coarse sieve, pressing on the solids to extract as much liquid as possible. Discard the pulp.

2. Return the corn cream to the saucepan, add the milk, and bring to a scald.

3. Meanwhile, combine the brown sugar, egg yolks, and bourbon in a large bowl and whisk just to blend.

4. While gently whisking the yolks, drizzle the hot cream mixture into them so that they are gradually warmed up. Return the mixture to the saucepan and set over medium-low heat. Cook, stirring with a wooden spoon (making sure that you are constantly scraping the spoon across the bottom of the pan), until the custard has thickened slightly and coats the back of the spoon.

5. Strain the custard through a fine sieve into a bowl and nestle it in a larger bowl of ice. Cool, stirring occasionally, then transfer to an ice cream maker and freeze according to the manufacturer's instructions. Transfer to a storage container and freeze until firm.

Makes 5 cups
Store for up to 2 weeks in the freezer.

Note: For "Chunky-Style" Corn Ice Cream, combine one-half cup sugar and one-quarter cup water in a small saucepan and bring to a boil. Add one-half cup corn kernels and cook for three minutes. Let cool, then strain the corn, discarding the liquid, and chill. Fold into the Corn Ice Cream while it is still soft, then freeze according to the manufacturer's instructions.

Piloncillo Ice Cream

Piloncillo is a flavor-packed raw Mexican sugar that is pressed into the shape of a pylon, hence the name. So what's a pylon? It's one of those big truncated cones that support bridges, OK? A big problem with these piloncillos is that they not only look like concrete pylons, they are also sometimes as hard as cement. Getting them to dissolve can be quite a job, so put them in a heavy plastic bag and give them a few friendly whacks with a hammer to break them up. See Mail Order Sources (page 209) for suppliers.

$1^1/_2$ cups milk

$1^1/_2$ cups heavy cream

4 ounces piloncillo, broken
   into pieces

$1/_4$ cup lightly packed dark
   brown sugar

9 large egg yolks

1. In a medium heavy-bottomed saucepan, combine the milk, cream, and piloncillo. Bring to a scald, stirring occasionally to dissolve the piloncillo.
2. Meanwhile, put the brown sugar and yolks in a large bowl and whisk just to blend.
3. While gently whisking the yolks, drizzle the hot cream mixture into them so that they are gradually warmed up.
4. Return the mixture to the saucepan and set over medium-low heat. Cook, stirring with a wooden spoon (making sure that you are constantly scraping the

spoon across the bottom of the pan), until the custard has thickened slightly and coats the back of the spoon.

5. Strain the custard through a fine sieve into a bowl and nestle it in a larger bowl of ice. Cool, stirring occasionally, then transfer to an ice cream maker and freeze according to the manufacturer's instructions. Transfer to a storage container and freeze until firm.

Makes about 1 quart
Store for up to 2 weeks in the freezer.

Banana Chocolate Crackle Ice Cream

Crackles of chocolate are far better than chips because they crunch and then melt in your mouth, releasing all of their wonderful flavor. To make them, drizzle melted chocolate into cold ice cream, instantly hardening it into thin squiggles. Make sure that your bananas are soft and ripe with a smattering of black freckles and a perfume that says "banana." They should not be stringy, watery, or sour-smelling.

$1^1/_2$ cups milk

$1^1/_2$ cups heavy cream

$2^1/_4$ cups sugar

9 large egg yolks

2 large bananas

4 ounces semisweet chocolate,
   coarsely chopped

1. In a medium heavy-bottomed saucepan, combine the milk, cream, and 1 tablespoon of the sugar. Bring just to a scald.
2. Meanwhile, put $1^1/_2$ cups of the sugar and the egg yolks in a large bowl and whisk just to blend.
3. While gently whisking the yolks, drizzle the hot cream mixture into them so that they are gradually warmed up. Return the mixture to the saucepan and set over medium-low heat. Cook, stirring with a wooden spoon (making sure that you are constantly scraping the spoon across the bottom of the pan), until the custard has thickened slightly and coats the back of the spoon.
4. Strain the custard through a fine sieve into a bowl and nestle it in a larger bowl

of ice. Cool, stirring occasionally, then refrigerate for at least 3 hours.

5. In a medium bowl, using an electric mixer or a wooden spoon, mash the bananas with the remaining sugar ($1/2$ cup plus 3 tablespoons) until they become soupy. Stir the mashed bananas into the chilled ice cream base, transfer to an ice cream maker, and freeze according to the manufacturer's instructions.

6. Meanwhile, melt the chocolate in the top of a double boiler over simmering water or a small bowl set over a saucepan of just-simmering water. Remove from the heat and let the chocolate cool, but don't let it harden.

7. Transfer the ice cream to a large chilled bowl. While folding it with a rubber spatula, drizzle the melted chocolate into it through the holes of a slotted spoon. Transfer to a storage container and freeze until firm.

Makes a little more than 1 quart
Store for up to 2 weeks in the freezer.

Peanut Butter Fudge Ice Cream

Chunks of fudge brownie smooshed into creamy peanut butter ice cream could get any cowpoke to holler "Yummy-Ki-Ki-Yummy-Ki-Ay!" You can use any leftover chocolate cake for this, but a plain, intensely chocolaty brownie works best.

1 1/2 cups milk
1 1/2 cups heavy cream
1 1/4 cups sugar
9 large egg yolks
1 cup smooth peanut butter

1 recipe Mexican Brownies
(page 134), made without
the raisins, coffee, pumpkin
seeds, and cinnamon,
chopped into 1/2-inch chunks

1. In a medium heavy-bottomed saucepan, combine the milk, cream, and 1 tablespoon of the sugar. Bring to a scald.

2. Meanwhile, put the remaining sugar (1 cup plus 3 tablespoons) and the egg yolks in a large bowl and whisk just to blend. Put the peanut butter in a medium bowl and set aside.

3. While gently whisking the yolks, drizzle the hot cream mixture into them so that they are gradually warmed up. Return the mixture to the saucepan and set over medium-low heat. Cook, stirring with a wooden spoon (making sure that you are constantly scraping the spoon across the bottom of the pan), until the custard has thickened slightly and coats the back of the spoon.

4. Strain about one quarter of the custard into the peanut butter and whisk to

blend. Strain in the remainder and whisk until smooth. Nestle the peanut custard in a larger bowl of ice. Cool, stirring occasionally, then transfer to an ice cream maker and freeze according to the manufacturer's instructions.

5. Transfer the ice cream to a chilled bowl. Fold the chopped brownies into the ice cream. Transfer to a storage container and freeze until firm.

Makes 1¹/₂ quarts
Store for up to 2 weeks in the freezer.

Serrano (or Jalapeño) Ice Cream

Serrano chiles are about half the size of jalapeños but have twice the bite. I prefer the pure flavor of serranos, but they are difficult to find, and jalapeños work fine in this recipe. Don't be nervous about this ice cream being too spicy; candying the chiles takes a lot of the heat out.

1 medium serrano or jalapeño chile	1 1/2 cups heavy cream
1 cup water	9 large egg yolks
1 3/4 cups sugar	1 tablespoon framboise
1 1/2 cups milk	(see Note)

1. Quarter the chile lengthwise and remove the seeds, veins, and any remnants of stem. Chop it into 1/4-inch pieces.

2. Place the chopped chile in a small saucepan, add the water and 1 cup of the sugar, and bring to a gentle boil over medium-low heat. Cook for 10 minutes, then remove from the heat and let stand for at least 4 hours.

3. In a medium heavy-bottomed saucepan, combine the milk, cream, and 1 tablespoon of the sugar. Bring to a scald.

4. Meanwhile, put the remaining sugar (1/2 cup plus 3 tablespoons), the egg yolks, and framboise in a large bowl and whisk just to blend.

5. While gently whisking the yolks, drizzle the hot cream mixture into them so that

they are gradually warmed up. Return the mixture to the saucepan and set over medium-low heat. Cook, stirring with a wooden spoon (making sure that you are constantly scraping the spoon across the bottom of the pan), until the custard has thickened slightly and coats the back of the spoon.

6. Strain the custard through a fine sieve into a bowl and nestle it in a larger bowl of ice. Let cool, stirring occasionally, then transfer to an ice cream maker and freeze according to the manufacturer's instructions.

7. Drain the chile and add to the soft ice cream. Transfer to a storage container and freeze until firm.

Makes about 1 quart
Store for up to 2 weeks in the freezer.

Note: Framboise, raspberry eau-de-vie, is available at better liquor stores. If you can't find it, substitute vanilla extract.

Brown Sugar-Vanilla Ice Cream

In 1520, Montezuma, the evil but glamorous Aztec emperor, greeted Hernando Cortés with a delicious drink of *chocolatl*—chocolate, honey, and vanilla. Cortés loved the concoction, but still had Montezuma summarily executed (garnering mixed, but enthusiastic reviews among the locals). The stuff quickly became the rage with aristocratic "foodies" back in Europe. Some eighty years later, a British apothecary discovered that vanilla didn't need any help from chocolate or honey; it was pretty yummy on its own. Today it is the foremost dessert flavor in the world.

1¹/₂ cups milk
1¹/₂ cups heavy cream
¹/₄ cup granulated sugar
1 vanilla bean, split

1 cup lightly packed light
brown sugar
9 large egg yolks
1 teaspoon vanilla extract

1. Combine the milk, cream, and granulated sugar in a medium, heavy-bottomed saucepan. Scrape the seeds from the vanilla bean into the mixture and add the bean. Bring to a scald over low heat.

2. Meanwhile, put the brown sugar, egg yolks, and vanilla extract in a large bowl and whisk just to blend.

3. While gently whisking the yolks, drizzle the hot cream mixture into them so that they are gradually wrmed up. (Leave the vanilla bean in the saucepan.) Return the mixture to the saucepan and set over medium-low heat. Cook, stirring with a

wooden spoon (making sure that you are constantly scraping the spoon across the bottom of the pan), until the custard has thickened slightly and coats the back of the spoon.

4. Pour the custard, with the vanilla bean, into a bowl. Let cool to room temperature and refrigerate until chilled.

5. Strain the custard through a fine sieve and freeze in an ice cream maker according to the manufacturer's instructions. Transfer to a storage container and freeze until firm.

Makes about 1 quart
Store for up to 2 weeks in the freezer.

Canela Ice Cream

Remember Red Hots, those spicy little cinnamon candies? Well, that's the flavor of canela, or "Mexican cinnamon." If you can't find it, then add the tiniest pinch of cayenne pepper and two more tablespoons of sugar to the milk and cream.

$1^{1}/_{2}$ cups milk

$1^{1}/_{2}$ cups heavy cream

2 ounces canela sticks

$^{3}/_{4}$ cup sugar

9 large egg yolks

1. In a medium heavy-bottomed saucepan, combine the milk, cream, canela, and $^{1}/_{4}$ cup of the sugar. Bring to a scald over low heat.

2. Meanwhile, put the remaining $^{1}/_{2}$ cup sugar and the egg yolks in a large bowl and whisk just to blend.

3. While gently whisking the yolks, drizzle the hot cream mixture into them so that they are gradually warmed up. (Leave the canela in the saucepan.) Return the mixture to the saucepan and set over medium-low heat. Cook, stirring with a wooden spoon (making sure that you are constantly scraping the spoon across the bottom of the pan), until the custard has thickened slightly and coats the back of the spoon.

4. Pour the custard, with the canela, into a bowl. Let cool to room temperature. Refrigerate until cool.

5. Strain the custard through a fine sieve and freeze in an ice cream maker according to the manufacturer's instructions. Transfer to a storage container and freeze until firm.

Makes about 1 quart
Store for up to 2 weeks in the freezer.

Mango Ice Cream

It's just a short walk down the block from the Alamo to the Menger Hotel. That's where everyone in San Antonio, from vacationers and residents to visiting presidents, goes to enjoy a dish of smooth mango ice cream, a Texas favorite.

1 1/2 cups milk
1 1/2 cups heavy cream
1 cup sugar

9 large egg yolks
2 ripe mangoes, peeled and
    sliced (see Note)

1. In a medium heavy-bottomed saucepan, combine the milk, cream, and 1 tablespoon of the sugar. Bring just to a scald.

2. Meanwhile, put the remaining sugar (3/4 cup plus 3 tablespoons) and the egg yolks in a large bowl and whisk just to blend.

3. While gently whisking the yolks, drizzle the hot cream mixture into them so that they are gradually warmed up. Return the mixture to the saucepan and set over medium-low heat. Cook, stirring with a wooden spoon (making sure that you are constantly scraping the spoon across the bottom of the pan), until the custard has thickened slightly and coats the back of the spoon.

4. Strain the custard through a fine sieve into a bowl and nestle it in a larger bowl of ice. Cool, stirring occasionally.

5. Meanwhile, puree the mangoes in a food processor fitted with the metal blade.

6. Whisk the mango puree into the cooled custard. Transfer to an ice cream maker

and freeze according to the manufacturer's instructions. Transfer to a storage container and freeze until firm.

Makes about 1 quart
Store for up to 2 weeks in the freezer.

Note: There's more than one way to cook a goose and at least two ways to skin and slice a mango. I think that this is the easiest: Hold the mango flat in the palm of one hand and peel the skin off the top flat side. Now slice the flesh away from the pit, avoiding the tough "hair" that clings to the pit. Flip the mango over and repeat the procedure on the other side.

Sweet Potato Ice Cream

Strange as it sounds, Native American sweet potatoes are in the morning glory family. Although they are very often called yams, they have nothing to do with those giant African roots; true yams very rarely make appearances in our markets. Honey is the catalyst that brings out the flavor of sweet potato in this ice cream.

$1^1/_2$ cups milk
$1^1/_2$ cups heavy cream
$^3/_4$ cup sugar
9 large egg yolks

$^1/_4$ cup honey
One $^3/_4$-pound sweet potato,
   peeled and cut into 8 pieces

1. In a medium heavy-bottomed saucepan, combine the milk, cream, and 1 tablespoon of the sugar. Bring to a scald.
2. Meanwhile, put the remaining sugar ($^1/_2$ cup plus 3 tablespoons) and the egg yolks in a large bowl and whisk just to blend.
3. While gently whisking the yolks, drizzle the hot cream mixture into them so that they are gradually warmed up. Return the mixture to the saucepan and set over medium-low heat. Cook, stirring with a wooden spoon (making sure that you are constantly scraping the spoon across the bottom of the pan), until the custard has thickened slightly and coats the back of the spoon.
4. Strain the custard through a fine sieve into a bowl and stir in the honey. Nestle the bowl in a larger bowl of ice. Cool, stirring occasionally.

continued

5. Meanwhile, bring a large saucepan of water to a boil, add the sweet potato, and cook until tender. Drain well, and mash the sweet potato with a fork or food mill until smooth. Let cool.

6. Whisk the mashed sweet potato into the chilled custard, transfer to an ice cream maker, and freeze according to the manufacturer's instructions. Transfer to a storage container and freeze until firm.

Makes a little more than 1 quart
Store for up to 2 weeks in the freezer.

Root Beer Creamsicle

Vanilla ice cream surrounded by a tangy ice makes that old summertime favorite, the creamsicle. The standard version uses an orange ice; this one is based on another soda fountain classic, the root beer float.

¹/₂ recipe Brown Sugar–
Vanilla Ice Cream
(page 160) or 1 pint
vanilla ice cream

¹/₂ recipe Root Beer Ice
(page 174)

With a small ice cream scoop, scoop out a ball of ice cream the size of a walnut and drop it onto the ice. Push the ice cream across the ice, scraping up the ice around it. Twist and wiggle the ball to evenly coat it on all sides. You should end up with a ball twice as big as the original ice cream ball. (If you prefer, start with larger balls of ice cream and end up with fewer but bigger scoops.) Serve immediately in an ice cream dish.

Serves 6 to 8
Keep frozen on a tray for up to 2 hours.

ICES

Fire and Ices

Because they contain less sugar, old-fashioned American ices are fresher-tasting and livelier than highfalutin European sorbets. They have a delightful, grainy texture that releases their flavor in bursts, and they don't have to be made in an ice cream machine. All you need is a shallow nonreactive pan, an ice pick or a fork, and your freezer.

Cinnamon Ancho Ice

The process of tasting food is a little more complicated than chomping down and saying yummy (or yech, as the case may be). Due to concentrations of taste buds and other nerve sensors, parts of your mouth are more sensitive than others. These ices really accent them. First a burst of sweet cinnamon hits the tip of your tongue. Then your whole mouth is chilled in a cooling bath of musky ancho. Finally, as you swallow, a little burst of fire explodes at the back of your throat.

4 cups water
1³/₄ cups sugar
3 ounces cinnamon sticks

1 tablespoon plus 1 teaspoon
  ancho powder (see Mail
  Order Sources)
¹/₈ teaspoon cayenne

1. Combine all of the ingredients in a medium saucepan and bring to a boil over medium heat. Continue to cook for 5 minutes more, then remove the syrup from the heat and set aside to cool.

2. Strain the syrup into a medium bowl and let it sit for 15 minutes until the sediment settles on the bottom. Taking care to leave the gritty sediment undisturbed, pour the clear liquid into a shallow 1¹/₂-quart, freezerproof container. Freeze for 8 hours, or until hard.

3. Just before serving, chop the ice into fine chunks and granules with a fork or multipronged ice pick.

Makes 1 quart
Store for up to 2 weeks in the freezer.

Burnt Orange Ice

The sweetness of orange and the rough edge of caramel are like a desert sunset—colorful, rugged, and gorgeous.

3 ounces (*¹/₄ cup plus 2 tablespoons) water*

1¹/₂ cups sugar
1 quart orange juice

1. Combine the water and sugar in a large saucepan and cook over high heat until the syrup turns a deep amber color. Turn the flame down to low, stand back and slowly drizzle half of the orange juice into the caramel. It will bubble up, and there may be splattering, so protect your hands with an oven mitt or towel. Cook for 3 or 4 minutes, swirling the pan, until most of the caramel chunks are dissolved. Add the remaining orange juice and stir to blend. Set aside to cool, stirring occasionally to help dissolve any stubborn caramel.

2. Transfer to a shallow 1¹/₂-quart freezerproof container. Freeze for 8 hours until hard.

3. Just before serving, chop the ice into fine chunks and granules with a fork or multipronged ice pick.

Makes a little more than 1 quart
Store for up to 2 weeks in the freezer.

Danger: Caramel Burns! Use Extreme Caution.

Tequila Ice

Tequila is distilled from the starchy cores of blue agave plants, grown in the Jalisco region of Mexico under strict government supervision. Frequently misidentified as a cactus, the agave is a succulent relative of the amaryllis. Choose a gold or "reposado" tequila for a rich, mellow flavor. Since alcohol inhibits freezing, I boil some of it off, but enough remains to impart the ice with the fine, soft texture of an Italian granita and a little tequila kick.

3 cups water
1 cup gold or "reposado"
  tequila

1 cup sugar
Juice of 1 lime

1. Combine the water, tequila, and sugar in a medium saucepan and bring to a boil over medium heat, stirring a few times to help dissolve the sugar crystals. Boil for 5 minutes, then remove from heat and let cool.
2. Stir the lime juice into the tequila syrup and transfer to a shallow 1½-quart and nonreactive, freezerproof container. Freeze for 8 hours, or until hard.
3. Just before serving, chop the ice into fine chunks with a fork or multipronged ice pick.

Makes a little more than 1 quart
Store for up to 2 weeks in the freezer.

Texas Pink Grapefruit Ice

Late winter is the season for sweet, tart Texas grapefruits, full of bright, pink juice that makes a great "pick-me-up" ice with a citrus jolt.

$^1/_4$ cup water
$^1/_2$ cup sugar

4 cups fresh pink grapefruit juice, preferably from Texas grapefruits, strained

1. Combine the water and sugar in a large saucepan and bring to a boil over medium heat, stirring a few times to help dissolve the sugar crystals. Remove from the heat and let cool.
2. Whisk the grapefruit juice into the sugar syrup, and transfer to a shallow 1$^1/_2$-quart freezerproof container. Freeze for 8 hours, or until hard.
3. Just before serving, chop the ice into fine chunks with a fork or multipronged ice pick.

Makes a little more than 1 quart
Store for up to 2 weeks in the freezer.

Root Beer Ice

The West is root beer country. Use a premium root beer, such as Soho or Stewart's. You can also try sarsaparilla as a substitute.

¹/₄ cup plus 2 tablespoons water

³/₄ cup sugar

Three 12-ounce bottles root beer

1. Combine the water and sugar in a large saucepan and bring to a boil over medium heat, stirring a few times to help dissolve the sugar crystals. Remove from the heat and let cool.
2. Whisk the root beer into the sugar syrup, and transfer to a shallow 1¹/₂-quart freezerproof container. Freeze for 8 hours, until hard.
3. Just before serving, chop the ice into fine chunks with a fork or multipronged ice pick.

Makes a little more than 1 quart
Store for up to 2 weeks in the freezer.

Vanilla Ice

This ice has the rich flavor of a good vanilla ice cream, but it's as light and refreshing as any fruit sorbet.

$3^{1}/_{2}$ cups water

1 cup sugar

1 tablespoon vanilla extract

1 vanilla bean, split

1. Combine the sugar, water, and vanilla extract in a medium saucepan. Scrape the seeds from the vanilla bean into the mixture, and add the bean. Bring to a boil over medium-low heat, stirring a few times to help dissolve the sugar crystals. Reduce the heat to low and simmer for 3 minutes, then remove from the heat and let cool. Remove the bean.
2. Transfer the sugar syrup to a shallow $1^{1}/_{2}$-quart freezerproof container. Freeze for 8 hours, or until hard.
3. Just before serving, chop the ice into fine chunks with a fork or multipronged ice pick.

Makes 1 quart

Store for up to 2 weeks in the freezer.

DESSERT SALSAS

Where the Pear
and the Cantaloupe Play

Salsas are cold relishes that we usually think of as accompaniments to savory dishes. All you need is some mint, jalapeño, fruit, and imagination, and you will have a lively addition to almost any dessert. Serve these salsas alongside a cake or over ice cream and custard. They are best when first made, but will keep in the refrigerator for a good twenty-four hours.

Strawberry-Almond Salsa

When you think of Texas, you don't necessarily think of strawberries, but every April there is a great big festival held in Poteet. Under the shadow of a six-foot-tall strawberry statue, tens of thousands of Texans feast on shortcakes, cheesecakes, and strawberry wine.

1 pint strawberries, rinsed,
* hulled, and quartered*
1/4 teaspoon minced serrano or
* jalapeño chile*
1 tablespoon chopped fresh mint

1 tablespoon amaretto
2 tablespoons sugar
1/2 cup (11/4 ounces) toasted
* sliced almonds*
* (see page xxi)*

1. Place half the strawberries in a large bowl, and add the chile, mint, and amaretto. Sprinkle on the sugar. Refrigerate for 20 minutes to 3 hours, tossing occasionally.
2. Just before serving, stir in the remaining strawberries and the almonds.

Makes about 1¹/₂ cups

Raspberry-Cherimoya Chip Salsa

With a flavor somewhere between pineapple, strawberry, and banana, the cherimoya has a seed-studded but custardy interior. Outside is a leathery green suit of armor that makes it look like a cross between a papaya and a Ninja Turtle.

1 large (*1/2-pound*) or 2 small
   cherimoyas
1 pint raspberries
1/3 cup (2 ounces) semisweet
   chocolate chips

1/4 teaspoon minced serrano or
   jalapeño chile
1 tablespoon chopped
   fresh mint

1. Slice the cherimoya(s) lengthwise and scoop out the creamy white flesh from each half. It should come out in one piece. Remove the seeds, either by picking them out one by one or by pressing the fruit through a nonreactive coarse-mesh strainer.
2. Taking care not to crush the raspberries, combine all of the ingredients in a medium bowl and toss gently to mix. Serve.

Makes about 1¹/₂ cups

Drunken Papaya Salsa

Technically a berry, papayas, which are packed with a digestion-aiding enzyme, are available almost all year long. Look for yellow-skinned fruit that yields slightly to the touch.

1 ripe papaya

$^1/_4$ teaspoon minced serrano or
jalapeño chile

1 tablespoon chopped fresh mint

1 tablespoon gold tequila

1 teaspoon lime juice

2 tablespoons sugar

1. Peel the papaya, slice it in half, and scrape out the seeds with a spoon. Cut the papaya into $^1/_2$-inch chunks.
2. Put half of the papaya, the chile, mint, tequila, and lime juice in a medium bowl. Sprinkle on the sugar and toss. Refrigerate for 30 minutes to 3 hours, tossing occasionally.
3. Just before serving, stir in the remaining papaya chunks.

Makes about 1$^1/_2$ cups

Melon and Blackberry Salsa

Lemon verbena is a yummy herb with a sharp citrus tang. To see what it tastes like, just gently suck on the leaves; chewing releases too much of the bitter flavor of the stems. Lemon verbena complements mild melons like Crenshaw, Canary, Golden Flesh, and honeydew. Try a little bit of minced serrano or jalapeño chile in this salsa, but go lightly to avoid overpowering the melon.

1 ripe melon
1 bunch ($^{1}/_{2}$ ounce) fresh
   lemon verbena (see Note)

1 pint blackberries

1. Halve the melon and remove the seeds. Cut it into wedges, slice the flesh away from the rind, and cut it into 1-inch chunks. Put the melon in a medium bowl.
2. Pick the leaves off the lemon verbena sprigs and lay them flat. With a small sharp knife, slice the leafy parts away from the center stems and finely chop. Sprinkle the lemon verbena over the melon and refrigerate for 10 minutes to 6 hours, tossing occasionally.
3. Just before serving, gently stir in the blackberries.

Makes 2 cups

Note: If you can't find lemon verbena, substitute mint.

Apricot-Hazelnut Salsa

Roasted hazelnuts and fresh apricots are two strong flavors that can both stand up to and complement each other.

*1 pound apricots, pitted and
  cut into 6 wedges each
$^1/_4$ teaspoon chopped serrano
  or jalapeño chile
1 tablespoon minced fresh mint*

*1 tablespoon Frangelico
2 tablespoons sugar
$^1/_2$ cup skinned and roasted
  hazelnuts (see page xxi)*

1. Combine the apricots, chile, mint, and Frangelico in a medium bowl. Sprinkle on the sugar and toss. Refrigerate for 20 minutes to 3 hours, tossing occasionally.

2. Just before serving, stir in the hazelnuts.

Makes 1¹/₂ cups

Apple-Walnut Salsa

Black walnuts grow wild in the Southwest. If you can find them and prefer their intense, slightly bitter flavor, go ahead and use them in this salsa. If not, regular walnuts will do just fine.

2 tablespoons unsalted butter
  or vegetable oil
1 pound Granny Smith apples,
  peeled, cored, and sliced into
  $1/2$-inch-thick wedges
$1/2$ cup sugar

$1/2$ teaspoon cinnamon
$1/8$ teaspoon cayenne
$3/4$ cup (4 ounces) toasted
  walnut halves or pieces
  (see page xxi)

1. Heat a large sauté pan over very high heat for 1 minute, then add the butter. Melt the butter, and swirl the pan to coat the bottom, then add the apple slices in a single layer. Sprinkle on the sugar and cook without stirring for 5 minutes. Add the cinnamon and cayenne and cook, tossing occasionally, for 3 minutes, or until the apples are evenly golden brown. Remove from the heat and let cool.
2. Just before serving, stir in the walnuts.

Makes 1$1/2$ cups

Chocolate Raspberry Salsa

Raspberries and chocolate have a sensuality all their own. Add some hot chiles, and anything can happen. Heat levels in jalapeños and serranos vary greatly, so taste as you go, adjusting accordingly.

1¹/₂ ounces bittersweet choco-
    late, finely chopped
¹/₂ cup heavy cream
1 pint raspberries

¹/₄ teaspoon chopped serrano
    or jalapeño chile
1 tablespoon chopped fresh mint

1. Put the chocolate in a medium bowl. In a small saucepan, bring the cream to a scald over medium heat. Pour half of the hot cream over the chocolate, and gently stir to melt and blend. Add the rest of the cream, and stir until smooth. Let cool.

2. Gently fold the raspberries into the chocolate mixture. Transfer to a serving bowl, sprinkle the chile and mint on top, and serve.

Makes 1¹/₂ cups

Grilled Pineapple with Caramel Sauce

This is a fun dessert that can be partially made outside. Make the caramel sauce ahead of time. Just before serving, flip the pineapple onto the barbecue to grill.

1 ripe pineapple (see Note)
1 recipe Clear Caramel Sauce
  (page 196)
2 tablespoons minced
  fresh mint

$^1/_2$ teaspoon chopped serrano
  or jalapeño chile

Vegetable oil for the grill

1. Prepare a hot fire in a barbecue grill.
2. Peel the pineapple and cut the little eyes out. Split it lengthwise into quarters and slice off the tough core. Slice each quarter into 3 long strips.
3. Lightly oil the grill rack. Grill the pineapple strips until grill marks appear on the bottom side, then flip them over and cook on the other side. Transfer to individual plates, and serve with the Caramel Sauce and a sprinkling of mint and chile.

Serves 6

Note: To test a pineapple for ripeness, try to pick it up by one of its center leaves. If it pulls out, then it is ripe. To test for flavor, turn it upside down and smell the bottom. The aroma should scream "pineapple"!

SAUCES

The Painted Dessert

Bright fruit sauces make Southwestern desserts look beautiful. Bold and colorful, they are as radiant as a sunset on the desert and always packed with the most important ingredient: fresh flavor.

Because we are full by the end of the main course, desserts have to look seductive. Why else, besides pure gluttony, would we want to eat them? With this in mind, European pastry chefs devised all sorts of methods for pulling sugar and molding chocolate into all sorts of figurines and doodads. Somewhere along the way they lost touch with the original idea: It's Food! After all, you wouldn't want to eat a piece of liver cooked until it turned rock hard and then molded into the shape of a cuckoo clock.

Tia Maria Chocolate Sauce

You can try Kahlúa or any other coffee liqueur in this sauce, but Tia Maria is a brandy with a unique and complex flavor.

*2 ounces bittersweet chocolate,
    finely chopped*

*¹/₂ cup heavy cream
¹/₄ cup Tia Maria*

Put the chocolate in a small bowl. In a small saucepan, bring the cream to a scald over medium heat. Pour half of the hot cream over the chocolate and gently stir to melt and blend. Add the rest of the cream and the Tia Maria, and stir until smooth. Serve slightly warm or at room temperature. (To reheat, set a container of the sauce in hot water and stir until warm.)

Makes 1 cup
Store for up to 2 weeks in the refrigerator.

Note: For a nonalcoholic sauce, replace the Tia Maria with an equal amount of cream.

Clear Mint Sauce

Plunging them into boiling water and then quickly cooling them in ice water sets the color of the mint leaves and rids them of their slightly oily taste. It's best to use a blender for this sauce; food processors just don't chop fine enough.

$^1/_2$ cup water

$^3/_4$ cup sugar

1 bunch (1 ounce) fresh mint

1. Combine the water and sugar in a small saucepan and bring to a boil over medium heat, stirring a few times to help dissolve the sugar crystals. Remove from the heat and let cool.
2. Pick the leaves off the mint and discard the stems. Dump the leaves into a saucepan of boiling water for 30 seconds, then quickly drain and plunge into a bowl of ice water to cool. Drain, then squeeze out any excess water.
3. Put the mint and sugar syrup in a blender and process until very smooth. Refrigerate until ready to serve.

Makes 1 cup
Store for up to 2 weeks in the refrigerator.

Mango Sauce

A good mango is golden to red in color and yields slightly when squeezed. Avoid any that are covered with brown speckles, have mushy spots, or are partially green. If your mango is too hard, store it away from light at room temperature until it ripens.

¹/₄ cup water　　　　　　　　　　　*1 ripe mango, peeled and*
¹/₂ cup sugar　　　　　　　　　　　*sliced (see page 164)*

1. Combine the water and sugar in a small saucepan and bring to a boil over medium heat, stirring a few times to help dissolve the sugar crystals. Remove from the heat and let cool.
2. Combine the mango and sugar syrup in a blender or food processor fitted with the metal blade and puree. Strain and refrigerate until ready to serve.

Makes 1 cup
Store for up to 1 week in the refrigerator.

Raspberry Sauce

To preserve their delicate flavor, the raspberries should be cooked very briefly, just enough so that they soften up and absorb the sugar. For an elegant finish, add a little framboise (raspberry eau-de-vie).

¹/₄ cup water
¹/₄ cup sugar
¹/₂ pint fresh raspberries or
1 cup individually quick-
frozen raspberries

1 tablespoon framboise
(optional)

1. Combine the water, sugar, and raspberries in a small saucepan and boil over medium heat, stirring a few times to help dissolve the sugar crystals. Remove from the heat and stir in the framboise, if using.
2. Strain. Let cool, then refrigerate until ready to serve.

Makes about 1 cup
Store for up to 1 week in the refrigerator.

Note: You can substitute blackberries in this recipe. Your sauce will be lovely.

Blueberry Sauce

Cooking releases the flavor and color locked in blueberry skins. It also releases pectin, the natural thickening agent that is used to make preserves and jelly.

¹/₂ cup crème de cassis
¹/₄ cup sugar

¹/₂ pint fresh blueberries or 1 cup individually quick-frozen blueberries

1. Combine the crème de cassis, sugar, and blueberries in a small saucepan and bring to a boil over medium heat, stirring a few times to help dissolve the sugar crystals. Reduce the heat and simmer for 10 minutes.
2. Strain the sauce through a fine strainer, making sure to press all of the juices out of the blueberry skins. Let cool, then refrigerate until ready to serve.

Makes 1 cup
Store for up to 1 week in the refrigerator.

Whiskey Butterscotch Sauce

I've seen recipes for butterscotch that use Scotch whiskey, so why not bourbon? It has a rich, round flavor that tastes luscious in desserts.

3/4 cup lightly packed dark
   brown sugar
1/4 cup bourbon
1 tablespoon vanilla extract

1 cup light cream
1 teaspoon cornstarch
2 tablespoons unsalted butter

1. Combine the brown sugar, bourbon, vanilla extract, and 3/4 cup of the cream in a heavy-bottomed medium saucepan and bring to a boil over medium heat. Boil for 5 minutes.
2. Meanwhile, whisk the remaining 1/4 cup cream and the cornstarch together in a small bowl.
3. Add the butter to the boiling cream mixture and swirl it around to blend. Whisk the cornstarch mixture and add it to the sauce. Cook, whisking for 2 minutes until thickened. Serve hot, or let cool to room temperature. (To reheat, set a container of sauce in a saucepan of hot water and stir until heated through.)

Makes 1 1/2 cups
Store for up to 1 week in the refrigerator.

Vanilla Custard Sauce

Crème anglaise, or pouring custard as it is traditionally called in the United States, is the perfect match for anything warm and chocolaty.

1/2 cup milk	*1/4 cup lightly packed light*
1/2 cup heavy cream	*brown sugar*
1 tablespoon granulated sugar	*3 large egg yolks*
1/2 vanilla bean, split	*1 teaspoon vanilla extract*

1. Combine milk, cream, and granulated sugar in a medium heavy-bottomed saucepan. Scrape the seeds from the vanilla bean into the milk mixture, add the bean, and slowly bring to a scald.
2. Meanwhile, put the brown sugar, yolks, and vanilla in a medium bowl and whisk just to blend.
3. While gently whisking the yolks, drizzle the hot cream mixture into them so that they are gradually warmed up. Return the mixture to the saucepan and cook over medium heat, stirring with a wooden spoon (making sure that you are constantly scraping the spoon across the bottom of the pan), until the custard has thickened slightly and coats the back of the spoon. Remove from the heat and let cool in a large bowl of ice.
4. Strain the sauce through a fine sieve and refrigerate until ready to serve.

Makes about 1 cup
Store for up to 3 days in the refrigerator.

Clear Vanilla Sauce

This speckled clear sauce makes a great syrup for pancakes or waffles.

1 cup sugar	*1 vanilla bean, split*
1/2 cup water	

1. Combine the sugar and water in a small saucepan. Scrape the seeds from the vanilla bean into the pan, add the bean, and bring to a boil over medium heat, stirring a few times to help dissolve the sugar crystals. Remove from the heat and let cool.

2. Strain the sauce through a fine sieve, and reserve the vanilla bean for another purpose (such as vanilla sugar or Vanilla Custard Sauce, page 194).

Makes about 1 cup

Store for months in a sealed jar at room temperature.

Clear Caramel Sauce

Always be very careful when handling caramel. It's extremely hot and temperamental—and may splatter.

1¼ cups water   *1 cup sugar*

1. Combine ¼ cup of the water and the sugar in a medium heavy-bottomed saucepan and cook over high heat until the syrup turns a rich amber color.
2. Reduce the heat to low, stand as far back as possible, and slowly drizzle the remaining 1 cup water into the caramel. It will bubble up and may splatter, so protect your hands with an oven mitt or towel. Swirling the sauce in the pan, cook for 3 to 4 minutes, until the caramel chunks dissolve. Remove from the heat and let cool.

Makes 1½ cups
Store for months in a sealed jar at room temperature.

Danger: Caramel Burns! Use Extreme Caution.

Pumpkin Sauce

We are used to a spicy-sweet taste in pumpkin desserts, but apple juice gives this deep orange sauce a fruity flavor.

³/₄ cup apple juice
¹/₂ cup sugar
¹/₂ cup pumpkin puree
  (canned is fine)

¹/₂ teaspoon cinnamon

1. Combine the apple juice and sugar in a small saucepan and bring to a boil. Remove from the heat and whisk until the sugar crystals dissolve.
2. Add the pumpkin puree and cinnamon, and whisk until smooth. Refrigerate until ready to serve.

Makes 1¹/₂ cups
Keeps up to 1 week in the refrigerator.

Cajeta

This thick and yummy goat's milk caramel sauce takes patience—it must be boiled down and reduced from one quart to one cup. Use a big pot and keep a watchful eye so that it doesn't burn or boil over. It takes a while to make, but, believe me, amigo, it's worth the effort. Goat's milk is sold at most health food stores.

2 tablespoons water

¹/₂ cup sugar

1 quart goat's milk

Small pinch of baking soda

1. Combine the water and sugar in a large deep heavy-bottomed pot and bring to a boil over high heat. Cook until the syrup turns a light amber color.

2. Taking care not to get splattered, add the goat's milk to the caramel; the caramel will sputter and harden, but then dissolve. Bring to a boil, then reduce the heat slightly and add the baking soda. Cook at a rolling boil, scraping the bottom of the pan with a whisk from time to time to make sure the sauce isn't burning. Cook until thickened and reduced to approximately 1¹/₂ cups. Strain through a fine sieve and let cool. Serve at room temperature.

Makes 1¹/₂ cups
Keeps for 1 month in the refrigerator.

Note: If the sauce becomes too thick after it cools, thin the cajeta out with sweetened condensed milk.

Whipped Cream

For whipped cream that holds lovely soft peaks, use cold cream and chilled equipment. Choose your flavorings to match your dessert.

1 cup heavy cream
1 tablespoon confectioners'
  sugar

1 teaspoon vanilla extract or
  1 tablespoon orange, coffee,
  or other liqueur

Using a chilled fine wire whisk or an electric mixer with chilled beaters, whip the cream until it has thickened and falls in globs from the whisk or beaters. Add the confectioners' sugar and extract or liqueur and whip until soft peaks form.

Makes 3 cups

Note: Oops, have you overbeaten your cream? It can be saved if it hasn't turned grainy and broken. Lightly whisk in an additional $1/4$ cup cold heavy cream until it looks nice and soft.

CANDY

Big Rock
Candy Mountain

Every chuck wagon pastry chef should have a few candies in his or her repertoire. No one can resist nibbling on fudge or buttercrunch. Candies are also grand for turning Plain Jane desserts into belles of the ball.

Fruit and Seed Chocolate Bark

Slow, careful melting will produce a smooth, shiny bark. I spread the chocolate out on a sheet of pliable acrylic, then flip it over once, cool, and peel the plastic off. If unavailable, line a baking pan with aluminum foil.

¹/₂ cup pecans, sesame seeds, and/or pumpkin seeds
4 ounces bittersweet chocolate, coarsely chopped

¹/₂ cup dried fruit (raisins, currants, or cranberries and/or chunks of cherries, apricots, and/or pineapple)

1. Set a rack in the middle of the oven and preheat to 350°F. Toast the nuts and/or seeds on a cookie sheet for about 5 minutes (or until you hear the pumpkin seeds pop for 1 minute, if using), turning the pan once for even toasting. Set the pan on a rack to cool.
2. Melt the chocolate in the top of a double boiler over barely simmering water. Remove from the heat.
3. Stir the nuts and/or seeds and dried fruit into the chocolate. Using an offset metal spatula, spread the chocolate mixture in a ¹/₄-inch-thick even layer over the plastic sheet or a foil-lined baking pan until set.
4. Peel off the plastic, and break into serving pieces.

Makes about ¹/₂ pound
Store for up to 1 week in an airtight container.

Buttercrunch

It's fun to just slurp on a chunk of buttercrunch, but I like it best of all chopped up and sprinkled on ice cream.

*Melted butter or nonstick
   vegetable spray for greasing
   the pan*
¹/₄ cup heavy cream
4 tablespoons unsalted butter

*1¹/₄ cups lightly packed light
   brown sugar*
1 tablespoon bourbon
1 teaspoon vanilla extract

1. Lightly grease a 9-by-13-inch baking pan.

2. Combine the cream, butter, and brown sugar in a small heavy-bottomed saucepan and bring to a boil over high heat, stirring occasionally to help dissolve the sugar. Cook until the syrup reaches 285°F on a candy thermometer. Remove from the heat and carefully stir in the bourbon and vanilla, then pour into the prepared pan, letting it spread out in an even layer. Let cool.

3. If using as a topping break the buttercrunch into chunks, and grind in a food processor fitted with a metal blade. You want it to be the consistency of fish tank gravel.

Makes 1¹/₂ cups
Store for up to 1 week in a tightly sealed jar.

Strawberry Lollipops

Caramel-coated berries on a stick are adorable, but check the weather forecast: They will hold nicely on a dry day, but don't attempt them in high humidity as they may melt. You must work quickly once the caramel is ready, so set everything up in advance and dip the berries while the caramel is still liquid.

6 large strawberries
1/4 cup water

1 cup sugar

Six 6-inch bamboo skewers

1. Rinse and thoroughly dry the berries, if necessary, and spear each one on a wooden skewer. Place a loaf pan on top of a piece of waxed paper or foil.
2. Combine the water and sugar in a medium heavy-bottomed saucepan and bring to a boil over high heat. Cook until the syrup turns a light golden amber. Immediately remove from the heat and, working quickly, carefully dip each berry into the caramel to coat. Lay the lollipops across the top of the loaf pan so the strawberries hang over the side and any excess caramel drips onto the waxed paper or foil.

Makes 6 lollipops

Danger: Caramel Burns! Use Extreme Caution.

Chocolate-Cherry-Pecan Fudge

Fudge syrup loves to go wild and boil up out of the pot as soon as you turn your back. Be ready to lower the heat at a moment's notice.

Vegetable oil or nonstick
  vegetable spray for greasing
  the pan
3/4 cup milk
2 cups sugar
2 ounces unsweetened
  chocolate
4 tablespoons (1/2 stick)
  unsalted butter

2 teaspoons instant espresso
  powder dissolved in 1 teaspoon hot water
1/2 cup (2 3/4 ounces) toasted
  pecan pieces (see page xxi)
1/2 cup (2 3/4 ounces) dried
  sour cherries

1. Lightly grease a 9-by-13-inch baking pan.
2. Combine the milk, sugar, and chocolate in a medium heavy-bottomed saucepan and bring to a boil over high heat, stirring with a wooden spoon a few times to help dissolve the sugar crystals. Cook until the mixture registers 236°F on a candy thermometer. Remove from the heat, and stir in the butter until melted. Stir in the espresso, pecans, and dried cherries.
3. Pour the fudge into the prepared pan, spreading it evenly with a metal spatula. Let set, then cut into 1 1/2-inch squares.

Makes 4 dozen 1 1/2-inch squares
Store for 3 to 4 weeks, well wrapped, at room temperature.

Strawberry-Blueberry Leather

Sometimes called fruit roll-ups, leathers are easy to make. They consist solely of pureed fruit and a little sugar, slowly baked in an oven with a partially opened door. Mixing two different purees in a splashed Jackson Pollock pattern creates a sensational look as well as a great flavor combination. Leathers are reminiscent of jerky, the air-dried and cured meat that has always been so popular among the inhabitants of the Southwest.

1 pint strawberries, rinsed and hulled

1/4 cup plus 2 tablespoons sugar

3 tablespoons water

1/2 pint blueberries

1. Preheat the oven to 175°F.
2. Puree the strawberries with 1/4 cup of the sugar in a food processor fitted with the metal blade until completely liquefied.
3. Combine the water, the remaining 2 tablespoons sugar, and the blueberries in a small saucepan and bring to a boil over medium heat. Cook, whisking occasionally to help break up the berries, for 5 minutes, or until syrupy-looking. Remove from the heat and strain through a fine-mesh sieve.
4. Spread the strawberry puree in an even 1/8-inch-thick layer onto a nonstick 12-by-18-inch baking sheet or jelly-roll pan. Drizzle the blueberry puree in a free-

form pattern on top. Bake with the oven door slightly ajar for 50 minutes, or until solidified and no longer sticky. Transfer to a rack to cool.

5. Starting at one edge, carefully peel the leather off the cookie sheet. Cut it into shapes, or place it on a large sheet of plastic wrap and roll it up like a scroll.

Makes one 12-by-18-inch sheet
Store for up to 1 month in an airtight container at room temperature.

Note: If the leather gets too hard and dry, put it in the refrigerator overnight and it will soften up and become pliable again.

Mail Order Sources

Chiles and other Mexican and Southwestern products

Los Chileros
P.O. Box 6215
Santa Fe, NM 87502
(505) 471-6967

The Chili Emporium
328 San Felipe Rd. NW
Albuquerque, NM 87104
1-800-766-4568

Great Southwest Cuisine Catalog
630 West San Francisco
Santa Fe, NM 87501
1-800-872-8787

Kitchen Market
218 Eighth Ave.
New York, NY 10011
(212) 243-4433

Simply Southwest by Mail
7404 Menual NE
Albuquerque, NM 87110
1-800-447-6177

Baking Supplies, Nuts, and Dried Fruit

American Spoon Foods
411 East Lake St.
Petoskey, MI 48235
(616) 526-8628
(nuts and dried fruit)

A.L. Bazzini Co., Inc.
339 Greenwich St.
New York, NY 10013
(212) 334-1280 (8:30 A.M.–
   5:00 P.M. EST)
(nuts and dried fruit)

Chocolate Gallery, Inc.
56 West 22nd St.
New York, NY 10011
(212) 675-2253
*(equipment, cookie cutters, 22K
 gold dust)*

Maid of Scandinavia
3244 Raleigh Ave.
Minneapolis, MN 55416
1-800-328-6722

White Mountain Freezer Co.
800 E. 101 Terrace
Kansas City, MO 64131
1-800-343-0065

Zabar's
2245 Broadway
New York, NY 10024
(212) 787-2000 (9:00 A.M.–
 5:00 P.M. EST)

Index

216